The Glass Jar City

Stories From the Fight to Save Reading, Pennsylvania

By Matthew Shaner

Introduction

All great stories have a catalyst, a moment where the author finds the light of inspiration, putting pen to paper or hands to keyboard. This story started in February of 2009. I was in my fifth year working at a major investment company located in the Philadelphia suburbs. We were the main office of the corporation and a sprawling complex of buildings, art deco design, and so much money. I had moved millions of dollars of investments on a daily basis.

One morning, walking into the break room next to our work area, I noticed the counter was empty. I put my lunch in the refrigerator and went to my desk. A company-wide email waited on the computer. They had taken away paper cups in an effort to save money, encouraging us to bring in mugs and thermoses. We had a meeting that afternoon and the supervisor told us that, if they were taking away our cups, bad things were coming.

In mid-February another email went out to the company. They were holding meetings with human resources throughout the day. A friend of mine had her meeting in the morning and called me from her cell phone saying she was at home. They were staggered lay-offs. At lunch, the CEO sent a video message saying that, if you were still employed by the end of the day, you would be part of the next step of the company.

I waited.

Just before two in the afternoon, my meeting invitation arrived. I had fifteen minutes of employment left. There is nothing like knowing you are about to lose your job. I paced the office, talked to those I liked and respected, and prepared myself for the impact that still felt surreal.

The meeting was a room full of employees across different teams and branches. They told us we were finished, that we would get severance based on our experience and assistance with a job placement agency. I took the paperwork, collected my things, and drove home. I walked into our house to find my wife Valerie and our son Carter playing on the floor. I picked him up, hugged him, and broke down in tears. He was six months old. We had just purchased a row home outside of the city of Reading, Pennsylvania. The floor had fallen from under our feet.

In the span of a day, I had become a statistic. Millions of people lost their jobs that year as the economy crashed and the recession started. I collected unemployment benefits and placed Carter on Medicaid insurance. I spent days looking in the mirror and wondering what face stared back. Like many of those who lost their jobs, I returned to school for a new career path.

In 2011 a headline from the *New York Times* proclaimed Reading the poorest city in the country with a population over 65,000 people. Census data had revealed almost 45% of the city's residents living at the poverty line. This wasn't Detroit or Flint,

Michigan. This wasn't Camden or Philadelphia. This wasn't some city out there on a map that only existed in a news clip.

It was the place we drove by every day running errands.

In the years after 2012, I completed graduate school for creative writing. I had found my way into the healthcare field working in an emergency room doing patient registration. My thesis novel was a story of baseball, family conflict, dealing with the past, and understanding grace. After graduation, I looked in the mirror and asked myself the same question as I did in 2008.

Now what?

I knew that I wanted my writing to make a difference. What if I could make a difference now and not worry about my fiction topping a bestseller list? What if writing could be social service? What if it could be activism, an advocate for those who needed it the most?

The idea came to me in the summer of 2014.

Tell the story of Reading.

I started digging online, finding resources and contacts across the city. My first fifteen emails went out to churches because, I thought, who better to talk about fighting poverty and helping people? All fifteen went unanswered.

The guys at Hope Rescue Mission broke the trend and invited me over for a tour. As I met with them, the stories started to unfold. I talked with men struggling with homelessness, redefining their lives and getting on their feet. As I left that afternoon, I knew it would not be the last time I visited the Mission. Other contacts started to respond. The calendar filled.

People wanted to talk.

I crossed the city meeting with those on the front lines, individuals leading outreach organizations on tight budgets with overworked volunteer staff. I started working higher up the ladder of power and influence, meeting with Kevin Murphy. Murphy is the president of the Berks Community Foundation and oversees more than $60 million dollars in grant money that gets distributed to local applicants. He led me to Adam Mukerji, head of the Reading Redevelopment Authority, and former cabinet member of Governor Christie Whitman in New Jersey. These men thankfully offered additional connections and were vital to completion of this book. Each interview led to an additional one, to the suggestion of other places to visit and people to meet.

The story grew and changed on its own.

It took a conversation with Brian Kelly, head and sole paid employee of ReDesign Reading, to open my eyes. We were talking over a plate of pupusas in an El Salvadorian restaurant down the block from City Hall. Kelly is a graduate of the Wharton School of Business at the University of Pennsylvania. He's focused on bringing systematic change to the city and has ideas that may work as he moves to make them reality. He said, "There are three levels of poverty. The abject poor have no resources, income, or prospects. The working poor are trying, but the numbers don't work in their favor. The income insecure is almost half of the population. *If one member of the family loses income, the entire family will be on the street within six months."* The sentence was a sledgehammer.

We were one of the income insecure.

If, God forbid, Val or I lost our jobs we would be on the street in less than six months. This story wasn't out there somewhere. It was personal. It wasn't just the story of a city, it was our story. It was one of hope, of struggle and redefining identity.

The city of Reading, almost 250 years old, is now working through the fire. It is fighting to create a new image, to bring businesses downtown and educate its people to work in them. It has seen the very bottom and, I believe, will rise again to a new and better place. Reading serves as a valuable example to thinkers and strategists across this country. It is a template, a blank slate to form and shape with conservative and radical ideas to combat poverty. It is a testing ground, a battle ground, and a seeding ground.

As you read this book, you will be inspired. You will hear from the people driving Reading's development and progress. You will journey with me as we go deeper to uncover the truth about charity and outreach programs, their successes, failures, and conflicts.

This story is personal. It has changed my life and I believe it will change yours. My prayer is that this book makes a difference and that you will be a part of the difference, for words can truly change the world.

All opinions, unless otherwise noted, are those of the individuals being interviewed at the specific places and times stated in the text starting in the summer of 2014 and are reproduced here with their permission. Facts and figures, including demographics and specifics, are also connected to the time of their gathering and relevance to their specific point in the history of the city.

Chapter 1

Hope Rescue Mission

The city of Reading (pronounced Redding to locals) was founded in 1748, taking root by the planning efforts of Richard Penn, his brother Thomas, and Conrad Weiser. A strong German and Eastern European community settled in the area and the Pennsylvania Dutch influence is still felt today. The city became an important manufacturing center, with an iron industry surpassing that of England's at the time of the Revolutionary War. The city was used to detain Hessian prisoners in the early stages of the conflict. As the war ended, Reading continued to grow.

The Schuylkill Canal, completed in 1825, connected Reading to Philadelphia and the Delaware River. The Union Canal, completed in 1828, connected the Schuylkill and Susquehanna Rivers and the city of Reading to Harrisburg. These waterways became important modes of transportation until the development of the railroad system.

If you've ever played the classic version of Monopoly, you've seen Reading Railroad. It is named for the famous railroad founded in the city that operated for almost a century of prosperity. I did not know it at the time but, this railroad would play an important part in the very first organization that invited me over for a visit.

Val and I started attending Glad Tidings Church in Wyomissing in 2009. Glad Tidings holds two services on Sunday and one on Wednesday nights for youth. The church sees two thousand people come through its doors every weekend. The first Sunday of the month is Missions Sunday, with a message and offering focused on a specific local, national, or international outreach. We had sat through many services listening to the name of Hope Rescue Mission mentioned and, as I stared at my email wondering who to contact, Hope came into my mind.

I searched their website, found the general contact email, and fired off an interview request not knowing what to expect. I was still reeling from being ignored by the churches, and wondered if this book would get off the ground.

Robert Turchi, director of Hope, replied and offered to show me around.

Now, I'm not a huge fan of interviews. Job interviews always made me nervous. There's something about sitting across from an individual assessing your every word and action. This time, the experience would be flipped. I was the one asking the questions and, for that matter, what in the world would I ask?

At that point, I had the basic idea of the story. I wanted to know what Hope did and how it contributed to the fight against poverty. I debated scripting out questions, then decided against it. I would go in with a tablet and pen, meet the guys and have a normal conversation, noting anything of value.

This first interview also provided instant accountability. I could not, and would not, let them down. These people and organizations I'd meet wanted to get the story out there, to share what they are doing and how they are making a difference.

Reading is a unique experiment in social change. It is a city working on multiple levels to find and reclaim its identity. My visit to Hope Rescue Mission, the first on this journey, was a dramatic and powerful experience of a group dedicated to serve homeless men in Reading.

On a picturesque summer afternoon in late July 2014, I park outside of Hope Rescue Mission. The building sits in the northern section of the city, nestled just below historical homes and next to a strip mall. It is old and expansive; the entrance at the top of a large flight of steps that often prevented men to sick or physically unable to climb the stairs from entering the Mission. There was no ramp.

You climbed or you moved on.

A cross hangs high above the door. Men sit on benches outside the building engaged in conversation. They watch me as I enter the building.

The entrance opens to a large lobby with circular tables. A front desk attendant works to the left and large fans circulate air through the space, not providing much relief from the blanket of humidity outside. The woodwork and furnishings around the office are ornate and detailed, with awnings and staircase railings stained dark and moving in soft curves. I identify myself to the guy at the desk and he tells me to hang out as he makes a phone call.

Moments later, Robert Turchi and Frank Grill cross the lobby.

Turchi, a Philadelphia native, is the executive director of the Mission. He carries the size and presence of the former correctional officer that once patrolled Berks County Prison. He joined the Mission in 2011 and took over the role of director in 2013. His past carried him through service at Fellowship Bible Church of Philadelphia and as a Chaplain for the Philadelphia Police Department. For a man with law enforcement in his blood, his eyes are sincere. He knows every face that walks around us as we talk. He values every moment he spends with the men under his care and was in the midst of catching up from a week away in Virginia with his family.

As Turchi excuses himself to catch up on work, I shake hands with Frank Grill.

Grill, also a Philadelphia native, is the associate director of the Mission. His background is more corporate and he admits that his years in the business world were not the best. He had worked at Vanguard and PENN National Gaming in various operational roles. He found his way into volunteering at the Mission and, eventually, full time employment. He leads worship at Hopewell Christian Fellowship and, when he speaks, his voice lends easily to music. He's confident and charismatic, the presence of a man used to being on the stage whether in a conference room or in worship.

The current Hope Rescue Mission building was originally corporate property for the Reading Railroad. The Railroad would hold functions for its employees and their families in the various rooms and spaces. The CEO had an office in the area that is now a computer lab with two rows of donated desk top computers.

Employees could live at the building, socialize, and even use the bowling alley that once spanned the length of the lowest floor.

In 1894 the Mission was founded to help men of the city dealing with homelessness and the struggles of everyday life.

A door to the right of the lobby opens to the chapel and, as we walked through, Grill beams about the recent renovation of the space. The walls were sun yellow with rows of padded chairs facing a podium and stage. In the room where once the executives of Reading Railroad danced and celebrated, homeless men now meet nightly for chapel services. As one of the men works a broom in a far corner, Grill tells me about the services. They've had powerful evenings of revelation and worship, all staffed by volunteers from area congregations and the Mission itself.

He shows me the computer lab with carpeting donated by the, now closed, Willow Grove Air Force Base. Everything in the room is donated. As the chapel provides spiritual life, this room provides the connection to the businesses and organizations that may open doors to the real world. The men receive instruction in everything from job hunting to resume writing and navigating the digital universe.

We reenter the lobby and he shows me the sleeping area just off the entrance. In the winter months, when the city of Reading calls a Code Blue, the Mission opens its doors to help any men stuck in the cold. They create room in the lobby and use as much space as possible to provide food and warm beds.

The cafeteria is just past the sleeping area. This space also recently renovated with fresh paint and a new layout. Narcotics and Alcoholics Anonymous meetings are held there with in-house counseling services to residents in need.

Grill takes me to the kitchen. It is spacious, with equipment ready to feed a crowd that often swells over a hundred. The flooring tiles were donated by a pair of McDonald's restaurants. Food is gathered from local Wawa convenience stores, restaurants, and grocery stores. Breakfast is now free. Dinner still costs a dollar. Those residents who work and serve while living at the mission can eat three meals for free each day.

A young man appears wearing a red Ohio State University hat. Eddie, a resident at the mission, runs the kitchen.

"My mom called today," Eddie says.

"How long has it been?" Grill asks.

"Four years," Eddie replies. His voice catches.

"See what prayer can do?" Grill pats him on the shoulder and promises they will talk later. This is a place of miracles, a place that provides victory and, when you are struggling, any victory is one to be celebrated.

We leave the kitchen and make our way down a set of stairs to the Safe Haven living area. The space consists of sixty beds, each with a matching locked cabinet so belongings can be stored and not have to be carried around the city during the day. The beds sit over the lanes of the old bowling alley.

Grill tells me it was his job to plan the renovating of housing. He proposed room rates that could generate some income while teaching men valuable work skills. He had the idea, planned the space, and had no clue where they would get the furniture. As with other needs, the staff went to God.

"A lady from the Comfort Inn called one day. She said they were renovating all their rooms and asked if we needed furniture. I said we did and we sent out our donation trucks to get everything. Every room was outfitted completely. When God means us to have it, he will provide." We leave the housing area and head to the bathrooms. The rooms are painted white with exposed pipes and updated furnishings.

"Originally, we had four toilets and two showers for sixty guys and two of the toilets barely worked." He takes me around the corner, "One of our board members is the CEO of Essig Plumbing. He saw the situation and realized it wasn't going to work. He donated eleven new showers with tankless hot water heaters. Now every guy has a guaranteed hot shower."

We go to a room with donated medical equipment, shelving, beds, and tables. FaithCare, an organization normally functioning in third world countries, has agreed to operate a space within the

Mission. They will provide free medical care and clinic services. Reading Hospital, St. Joseph's Hospital, and Alvernia University have also joined the effort to offer medical assistance. Alvernia's Physical Therapy program will place students in the clinic space to provide free therapy as community service hours towards graduation.

The Mission serves the spirit and the body. They have a gym and basketball court. Grill tells me that some men volunteer to set up games for the residents. They have a holistic approach to growth and progress, a full effort to improve every area of life and provide a hand up and not a hand out.

I follow Grill through the building and he walks with purpose. We cross the gym space, our steps echoing around the room and shafts of light cut in through the antique windows. He leads me out of the building and across the back lot.

Gardens grow to our left. They provide enough vegetables for the Mission in the summer months. We cross the lot and approach a long, single-level building. This is a thrift store, warehouse, woodshop, and recycling businesses. A large mural adorns the side of the thrift store, painted by a young man now working part time in the woodshop.

The space is massive and filled with donated items. Displays are carefully organized and placed. There are rows of furniture, electronics, books, clothes, and jewelry. Grill points out refinished furniture, telling me that the woodshop has redefined the possibilities of what they could make and sell. The pride of the store is a cabinet shining under display lights and tagged at $300 dollars. If you transplanted it to a mainstream furniture store you would easily pay double. Grill tells me his house is more than half furnished by products he finds in the store.

We go through the warehouse, head back outside, and stop at the woodshop.

The room is stacked with works-in-progress.

I meet Mike, a man formally owning his own woodworking business, and now a resident of the Mission. He was in the midst of working on an antique ophthalmologist cabinet with twenty-five individual drawers. This was the guy revolutionizing the products of the thrift shop. He loved every minute of the sander, the finish, and the final result.

We walked back across the lot past a row of cars.

"Those cars belong to our residents," Grill tells me, "they work towards saving money and a car can go a long way to a job and their own residence." The entire building is a work in progress. Like the unfinished cabinet waiting for Mike's hand, the mission is consistently refaced and improved. Windows were being replaced on the second level in preparation for winter. Projects imagined and implemented. Discipleship classes held four nights a week offering training and valuable life skills.

As we return to the lobby, I ask about repeat residents. Grill tells me that some men have trouble seeing their situation. They rationalize and reason rather than recognize and address. They say they are moving in with girlfriends. They leave and, months later, return asking for new help.

"Are you a prayer warrior?" Grill asks me. He says that prayer is huge for these men as they face their addictions and issues.

The culture here is one of dignity, respect, and self-policing. Grill says that the cross on the door is known throughout the city. Hope is run with three full-time employees. The other roles are staffed by residents trusted and trained to help out. Every man I meet shakes my hand and smiles. The building resonates with inspiration. The guys in charge believe in their efforts and keep their eyes on the future.

Hope Rescue Mission, with all its years of existence, continues to be a beacon of light. It is a place working daily to make a difference in the city of Reading. They are always in need of help and time, mentors to meet with the men and serve on any level. The mission never stops and, for another century forward, it will continue to provide for any man climbing the steps and walking through the doors.

Hope Rescue Mission

645 North Sixth Street

Reading, Pennsylvania 19601

610-375-4224

www.hopeforreading.org

Chapter 2

Mercy Community Crisis Pregnancy Center

The Main Library branch of the Reading Library System, founded before the American Revolution, is an imposing building on a corner of 5th Street. It has columns and stone steps leading up to an entrance that houses a large collection of books. Across the street, in the shadow of the library, sits Mercy Community Crisis Pregnancy Center.

I found parking around the corner, up from a nail salon, a container and two bags of donations in my car for delivery. My wife had gone through clothes that both of our boys were too big to wear and sorted them the night before. As a father, children always hold the strings of my heart.

Sherry Camelleri, the executive director of Mercy meets me as I enter the building, a small lobby with a hallway and a waiting room off to the left. She leads me to the waiting room outfitted with a television, chairs, and toys for children.

"This was a doctor's office," she says, "and this was her waiting room." I follow her back through the first floor. Mercy is housed in a row of buildings, the entrance only differentiated by paint color and a white sign on the front. It opened in 1990. Camelleri shows me meeting spaces for parenting classes and storage areas for client files. In one classroom she points at the wall where a message board hangs on the wall with a verse of scripture written on it.

"Volunteers or staff can change the scripture verse as they feel led," Camelleri tells me. We go to a curving stairwell rising to a second and third floor. The stairs creak under our weight.

We stop in the resource room. It is a space with bins of clothes sorted by gender, size, and season. The clothes are cleaned and organized after donation. Clients can return once a quarter to select necessary clothing for their children and diapers and formula on a monthly basis, as available. "Never underestimate the importance of an item," Camelleri says, "We can't give it if we don't have it."

She points out a bin for socks that is empty at the moment.

"One day I was speaking with a client with a young child and now expecting a second one." They were in bad shape financially and considering abortion. "The lady needed a pregnancy test and also told me she needed three things for her toddler; a blanket, a winter coat, and a heavy sleeper. If the pregnancy test was positive, she was considering abortion because of their financial challenges. The pregnancy test was positive, with the client's permission, I prayed. Well aware that we did not have the items she requested, I prayed for God's intervention. Before going to the resource room, the doorbell rang. An older lady entered our building holding a bag, saying she was at home and felt prompted that she needed to give Mercy this donation right away. I took the bag and the lady left. I looked through it and found three things; a blanket, winter coat, and heavy sleeper, all the exact size the client needed. The client left with bag in hand and a changed outlook on her situation."

Abortion was no longer considered as her only option.

We walk through other rooms, all painted and outfitted with material and efforts from volunteers. She leads me to one with tables of white bags sorted by age groups.

"These are from our Christmas program last year."

In late fall, the parents sign-up for classes that teach valuable life skills. After completing their class, they can pick out gifts for children ages birth through eight. The program plans for 120 mothers and 300 children each year. The clients select gifts for their children and something for themselves and this gift, she says, normally ends up given to a valued friend or relative. All Christmas items are new and donated by local churches, individuals, and businesses.

"We've seen more families touched through this program than I can describe."

Mercy handles over 1,200 client visits a year. All services are provided free of charge. These include the parenting classes, supplies for prenatal preparation and the time directly after birth, and clothes as the children age and grow.

"Winter coats are so valuable," Camelleri says, "We had a family only sending one child to school a day because they had one heavy coat to go around. The others would stay home. Most people have coats for playing in the snow, holidays or church, casual winter stuff. Some families don't have a single winter coat."

We return to the first floor and take our seats in the waiting area.

"We seem to see a mix of prodigal sons and daughters and those never having set foot in the church." Mercy serves a range of ages, from young teen to nearing middle age. They will provide pregnancy tests if desired and refer people to service agencies in the city. As with all agencies, Mercy is a mandated reporter and hotline numbers for victims are available.

She swallows and her eyes soften. Mercy receives no outside funding from governmental sources, totally relying on God's provision.

Mercy's focus is on working with the whole person. Some of their clients lack the background of basic life skills and do not have a support system. They are in the midst of violent or ever-changing relationships. Imagine adding a child to the mix. The volunteers serving at Mercy often instruct parents to set examples for their children, that they have the chance to break the destructive cycles of their past and make a different future for the next generation.

"This volunteer experience doesn't work for everyone. Some go home and cry at night over the situations. We see broken lives, the very things that touch the heart of God. They need to have the right mindset. I'll tell you this, not one volunteer is unchanged by their experience. They must be willing to enter the world and see how God works and moves."

Mercy has seen an increase of women taking on children from their relatives or friends, even taking in their grandchildren.

When relatives and loved ones are lost to the street, life choices or jail, the children suffer. Mercy works to do everything they can to support these individuals, some navigating the journey of parenting alone. They recognize that every appointment is an opportunity to impact the heart and life of individuals and families in need.

I ask about young guys, if they ever come off the street looking for help.

"Of course," Camelleri replies. "We do what we can to help them. We've had gang members walk through the doors. They respect what we do because we provide services for their girlfriends, their children, or their sisters. This is a place of safety and peace." I remember myself as a teenager and wonder if I ever would have had the guts to enter a place like Mercy.

"As Christians, we are most comfortable with a front-door gospel. We can ring the doorbell and go through our tracks and memorize what we want to say. This place is not the front door. This is the house on fire. Firemen crawl in through the tight spaces to put out the flames. We must be willing to go in however we can, showing mercy, and the hope for a changed life through Jesus Christ."

As we talk, car radios pass the building blaring music in a mix of rap and Spanish melodies. Voices yell to each other. Phone calls are made. The street, and the city, is just beyond the door.

"You need to establish trust first. Our clients need to know they are not alone. We must earn the right to be heard. We can't just sit down and start talking about Jesus. We need to listen to their stories."

Stories are powerful. Mercy provides a service at the intersection of past and present. The volunteers connect with clients by sharing their own life stories. In a time where the past can provide so much pain, this place builds bridges of hope for the future.

"One day we had a guy in the waiting area. A few kids were playing on the floor and we had Veggie Tales cartoons on television. A volunteer noticed this guy had started crying. She went to the waiting room and asked him if he was alright." The man was an expectant new father. "He said the only memory he had of his father was watching Saturday morning cartoons and that he could do that but he was clueless as to everything else. This made him eager to start the parenting classes."

As we finish our conversation, I thank Camelleri for her time. She says that the stories in Mercy could fill an entire book. I tell her I needed to get my donation from the car.

I walk around the corner to where I had parked thinking about being a father, a man, and my responsibilities to my boys.

"Come back anytime and interview our volunteers." Camelleri tells me. She is proud of her clients and her staff of volunteers. She is proud of the referrals, most from word of mouth, leaving Mercy and flowing to all corners of the city. The families trust the staff. They know they are cared for, loved, and honored.

Before I walk away, I look at the building one final time. I think of the doctor who had originally lived there, seeing patients in the front and living on the upper floors. The building is on the National Historical Registry. There are still lives being saved, wounds being treated, and healing occurring on a daily basis so many years later.

Camelleri ushers me to the street and takes a breath.

"When I get to Heaven, I want God to tell me that I never missed an opportunity. I want him to say well done good and faithful servant."

Mercy Community Crisis Pregnancy Center

105 South 5th Street

Reading, Pennsylvania 19602

610-376-0828

www.mercypregnancycenter.org

Chapter 3

Greater Berks Food Bank

The first Sunday of every month at Glad Tidings church is focused on local, national, and international missions. They often play a short video to introduce the message. One video shows two women in split-screen, living in the city and the suburbs. They start their mornings attempting to make breakfast, one with food and one without. Both women realize they need to get groceries. The one with money drives to the store as the other walks to the local food pantry. At the store, as the woman's food goes down the cashier's belt, it crosses the line of the screen and is handed to the other at the pantry. The message is shaped for maximum impact and it works.

When I'd visited Hope Rescue Mission, I learned of the local businesses and people donating food. Hunger always seemed like a distant issue, until the first time I realized the supply of food at our home was running thin, that the boys needed meals the next few days and we didn't have much to give them. We couldn't afford to just go to the store and stock up.

The organization on the front line of the battle against hunger in Berks County is the Greater Berks Food Bank.

The Greater Berks Food Bank is a vital supply line for a large amount of programs, from food distribution in schools to pantries on the street. When I visited they were in the midst of switching to a new warehouse location that would double their storage space and vastly improve their reach.

Dinner around the table is a family tradition. We come home from work or school, talk about our days, and settle in for a meal. Now picture a family with empty cabinets and children waiting for some kind of sustenance. This is too great of a reality for many families in the city of Reading and the Berks County area.

Doug Long, Marketing and Development Manager, leads me in through the lobby as we dodge moving boxes and invoices. He is tall and thin, wearing the corporate casual uniform of a dress shirt and khakis. He ushers me through the office he has worked in for the last eight years, and into a conference room.

"In 1995," Long states, "we gave out a little less than 2 million pounds of food. Last year we gave out 7.2 million pounds." The organization is a storage and distribution facility for food donations from surrounding businesses and charities. They serve more than three hundred programs in Berks and Schuylkill counties.

"We go into Reading School District certain days and hand out a bag of fruit to every single student on their way home," Long tells me. In a city with almost half of its almost 90,000 residents below the poverty line, this effort can make a major difference, even with a trend moving in a surprising direction.

"Recently, we've tracked more need where you wouldn't expect it. Not in the city but in the suburbs with the 'working poor,' those families making nine or ten dollars an hour and struggling to put food on the table."

The Food Bank does not serve families directly, but they can call and be sent to a resource close to their location. I ask about the recession in 2008 and in 2011 when the bottom fell out of Reading's economy.

Long mentions they had seen a 40% increase in families using services over those years. Businesses had shut their doors and relocated, masses of workers were laid off, and those who provided for their loved ones were suddenly at home looking for replacement jobs. These families included children and Long's face is animated as he speaks about providing for the youngest ones in greatest need.

"Last year over 112,000 people accessed our services. That accounts for one in five residents of Berks and Schuylkill counties."

The Food Bank includes a department to examine the surrounding area and find underserved populations. They work with organizations, communities of faith, and other outlets to set up programs they can supply with food. It is building a web that flows with resources which can only come from willing donors.

"Over 80% of donations come from local donors like farmers, businesses, and community food drives. The remaining amount is supplied through some local and state resources," Long says. "Even with this assistance, we are still at the mercy of funding."

Government resources are divvied up by service area and the food bank must prove its worth and outreach abilities. Long justifies their funding with a simple illustration, "Any local home with five people, statistically, has someone impacted by the reach of Food Bank." Even with this knowledge, some smaller support organizations must fight to survive.

"We fight and make it work even when support dwindles. When the community suffers financially, it constricts giving." Hunger is a large hill to climb and connected with overall economic health. "There is always a need for education and job security."

Long's dream is that there would, one day, not be a need for a food bank to serve such a large group of people. Until then, the organization will keep gathering food and spreading it into the community.

The Food Bank relies on sixteen full time employees, a few temps, and over a thousand volunteers. They are in the process of moving into a new warehouse space which will cost $4.8 million dollars. The need is there as the food sits in the warehouse and the funding remains incomplete.

He takes me on a tour of the current space. There are rows of pallets stacked with food and a freezer loaded by forklift distributing a truckload of donations from a Hillshire distribution center above the city of Pottsville. The guys are struggling to fit the meat inside the freezer.

"You see how full that is?" Long asks. "Give it a week and we'll have it cleared."

Most families on a budget ignore the perimeter areas of a grocery store, the meats and produce, and center their efforts on the middle aisles. The middle aisles are all the processed food. They are not healthy but cheaper than the other options. The donations of meat and produce are like important for a family not having the option to buy their own.

The Food Bank moved over three million pounds of fresh and frozen goods last year. Wegman's, the supermarket chain, is one of the largest donors in the area. They often send multiple trucks with filled with produce that must be kept in cold storage. The new warehouse will provide a much larger cold storage unit. We walk through aisles of canned goods, cereals, and drinks, each section emptying and refilling weekly.

The Food Bank is a member of Hunger-Free PA and Feeding America, the associations of state and federal food banks. They will trade food if the need exists outside of their service area. All it takes is contact from a family or charity and deliveries will be arranged.

The current rotation of programs includes the Kids Café, an after-school program that provides meals to children in need. The Produce 4 Kids Program provides a bag full of fruits and vegetables for kids to take home at a select Reading elementary school on a given day (depending on the current volume of produce, two or three distributions may take place during a week). The Food Bank supports eighteen program sites throughout Berks and Schuylkill counties handing out 1,500 backpacks weekly. The Senior Food Totes Program provides a tote bag of food every month to more than

1,300 low-income seniors to supplement their current purchases with foods of high nutritional value.

An average of 45,000 people receives food monthly.

As I leave the warehouse workers are still moving and stacking food. They will be there late into the evening organizing multiple trucks of donations that had arrived that morning. The need is increasing, the economy is still struggling and the Greater Berks Food Bank continues moving food in and out on a daily basis.

There is hope to fuel the process.

When I arrive home, we have dinner. I sat across from Val and the boys and think of the other families doing the same with the help of the Greater Berks Food Bank and Doug Long's efforts, a vital link in the fight to reclaim the city of Reading.

Greater Berks Food Bank

117 Morgan Drive

Reading, PA 19608

610-926-5802

Chapter 4

Berks Coalition to End Homelessness

I kept having the same dream. There's a school of thought that believes repeated dreams are symbolic of our waking situations. I dreamt I was back as an undergraduate in college, even though I hadn't been for years. I was looking for a classroom to take a final exam and could not find it. Then I would check my calendar and realize I had missed the test.

I'd worry about missing the way out, as if this journey was some kind of highway and the off-ramp had already passed.

Some, in Reading, have no off ramp. They aren't moving, drifting through the days and fighting for survival. These numbers build and, when they hit critical mass, choices must be made. None are easy and progress always comes with a price.

The Berks Coalition to End Homelessness is the connection point for the majority of agencies operating within the city. Sharon Parker, Executive Director, plays many roles. She makes connections, polices disputes, oversees monetary movement and attempts to have all these agencies cooperate across the city with a population desperate for help.

I park in front of the Barnes and Noble and make my way to the entrance to find Parker waiting by the door. We exchange greetings, enter the store, and she hits the Starbucks while I find us a table.

"If we get a call for a need and we know a separate agency that can supply it, we connect the two," Parker tells me.

She laughs easily.

The Coalition started twenty years ago as three people getting together to organize and coordinate social services. The staff was entirely volunteers.

"Volunteering takes energy and, without a clear mission, it can die off," Parker says. The Coalition is unique in its connection to the Department of Housing and Urban Development (HUD). HUD requires a single agency in the city to take the lead for homeless services and they have stepped up to the challenge. A database of homeless individuals is maintained and statistics are tracked. They must prove the need for funds and follow a strict reporting process.

"We work well because we are all on board and work together for the families we serve," Parker says. Unity is a consistent theme. A combined effort is needed when tackling such a large problem. "I've had many churches call me with an idea to help the homeless. Charities are hard to start. I always ask them how much money they have. It is so much easier to join a movement already in progress, then to try and gain traction." Parker is a realist. "You know what the water bill is for the Hope Rescue Mission for the winter season? $18,000. They get no government funding. I tell churches that, if they want to make a difference, they should give money to Hope Rescue Mission and other places like it."

Their database also provides demographics of the homeless and tracks the individuals as they progress through the housing and social service system. It shows people who are repeated entries into the system and the flow of those moving from shelters to detox centers and transitional housing.

It paints a picture of the homeless experience.

"HUD says that homelessness is going down. They made a goal to eliminate it and, of course, they say it is happening. Here it is going up," Parker shakes her head. "It is like cleaning your desk. You can put everything in drawers and, guess what; the mess is still there, just out of site. That's how the government sees things."

Numbers do not equal faces.

I ask Parker what they have learned from their gathered data.

"Reading is over 60% Hispanic, so there are language barriers. The other issues are education and poverty. You want to fix homelessness? Train people to get jobs. When people emigrate from other countries, we have no idea about their educational background. We need to get them trained on job skills, free of health issues, and hired into paying employment."

The city is in need of large employers. Doors for jobs must be created and opened if the economic picture will ever change. Parker thinks for a moment.

"Did you know that there is no shelter in Berks County that will take in an intact family that is homeless?" The sentence repeats in my head. "Last December we had calls from fifteen families looking for services. Some were living in cars with young children. We had to split them. I ended up putting some in hotel rooms with my own money. I can't see these people back on the street."

I think about a family being told that they will be separated. Could I imagine leaving my wife and kids behind? You finally take the step to get help and find out it will not be together.

"If I had my dream, I'd have housing for families. It is a project we are working on right now with the Berks County Redevelopment Authority in the city. We actually found a building but it needs work and would end up with only three units. I need twenty units." Services for these families could be coordinated between outside agencies as they lived on site. "When I get the calls from families, I tell them to call their friends or relatives and ask if anyone would take them in, because we would have to split them up."

Parker tries to find the root cause of the problems for each client. She looks for solutions, even going the length of calling landlords and working out housing arrangements. Teenagers can present a unique challenge. If they are over twelve years old, they will be separated from their families when they enter the shelter system. U Turn, a service that specializes in teen mediation, will often get the first call.

"Teens don't want to go in shelter. They'd rather live with their friends or chance it on the street." The Coalition has contacted friends of kids in a search to find temporary shelter until the issues at home can be squared away. They follow the goal of holistic healing.

"We attack every issue. The homeless can be anywhere from infants to teens, adults, and the elderly. Elderly homelessness is a big problem. They end up not being able to pay their property taxes and find themselves on the street."

Police departments and hospitals often provide initial referrals.

"They normally just drop people off and leave. That doesn't help anyone. They know we are out there. Just call us. We will come to the ER and talk with patients who are homeless."

I tell her about my experience working in the emergency room and how we handled homeless patients. They could stay in the waiting room overnight if they were not bothering anyone, but they had to leave in the morning.

Parker sees opportunity in the midst of struggle.

"We have sixty people at our monthly meetings. We bring everything together. That is the key, having unity as we face down the problem of homelessness."

As we finish our conversation, there was a valuable opportunity. Every interview had yielded a powerful moment.

I realized the purpose for this book, the reason to tell this story.

It would be to make her project a reality, to donate funds from sales to help purchase housing for homeless families. It is important for the fight and the victory, for families facing down their struggles and for the final solution. We can eliminate the separation; allow families to remain a unit.

I mention it and her eyes light up.

"We need the stories of the people on the ground," she says, "I think it is a great idea."

Berks Coalition to End Homelessness

831 Walnut Street

Reading, PA 19601

610-372-7222

www.bceh.org

Chapter 5

Berks Women in Crisis

Poverty is not a singular issue. It impacts entire families and cities. It is passed from generation to generation in the absence of community resources. When poverty is added to psychological issues, from mental illness to anger management, a crisis situation will follow.

Everyone needs an outlet for their anger. Some people write, others talk to friends and family, and some will find a way to twist a negative into a positive and improve their lives. Watch the news any night of the week and you'll see the darker side. There are too many women, children, and even men living as victims of abuse by their loved ones.

"Oh you're going to talk to Women in Crisis?" my coworker asked. "I always donate to them."

We were standing in my office.

"In 1993, my best friend was murdered by an abusive ex-boyfriend. He had been stalking her, showed up at her work, and shot her in her car. The location of the funeral had to be concealed from the public because he threatened to show up and kill her entire family." Her voice cracked with emotion.

With this story fresh in mind, I called Christine Gilfillan, the Associate Director of Berks Women in Crisis.

Their new building, located on a corner just inside the city, looks like a small college dorm. It was built to combine different locations under one roof and increase the housing capacity from twenty-six to fifty people, three to four months in duration. The organization operates on a mix of public and state funding.

"We offer anything from temporary housing to legal services," Gilfillan tells me. Berks Women in Crisis has a small crew of lawyers to assist with obtaining restraining orders and navigating the tricky legal ground that comes with abusive relationships. The housing area of the facility is staffed twenty-four hours a day.

One of their biggest challenges is getting information out to the public.

"We'll go into schools, places of employment and community groups. We'll even do professional training for service providers," Gilfillan says. There is no budget for marketing and these presentations are often the only way a victim gets connected with help. Those in need are mostly women but, more often, they have assisted men in getting out of dangerous relationships also.

Gilfillan has worked for the agency for thirteen years.

"One in every four women is a victim of abuse," she says, "The poverty in this city only makes things worse." With poverty comes stress and struggle. When people can't handle the adverse conditions, violence flares in response.

All of the services offered are free and given without any income requirement. The majority of the clients are young adults.

"We are about providing the resources to get people out of their situations. Some, though, never make it out." I think of my coworker and her friend. "We'd love to expand everything, from housing to legal services. In an ideal world, there would be bases of support throughout the city so people can see the value of what we have to offer."

Their currency, on the streets, comes through education and information.

"There is a tendency for 'victim blaming' and we need to fight that," Gilfillan says. "People aren't eager to talk about their problems. It's hard to define success for our clients. We want them to make their own choices."

There are repeat clients, even with the counseling and legal services.

"Sometimes people go back to a bad situation on their own," Gilfillan says.

Referrals often come from the police department or local hospitals. A crisis response team will go to a specific location when needed, whether the hospital itself, a home, or even the court house.

Physical abuse is one result of the poverty that holds the city of Reading like a vice. Berks Women in Crisis offers a range of solutions to improve the lives of those who walk through the front doors. Stand in a room with five women and one, statistically, has been abused. Organizations like this are working to change that reality and they consistently operate on the edge of their budget.

After our interview, I'm still thinking about my coworker's story and how her friend was a victim. The depths and heights of this battle against poverty only increase as the journey continues.

Berks Women In Crisis

255 Chestnut Street

Reading, Pennsylvania 19602

610-373-1206

www.berkswomenincrisis.org

Chapter 6

Service Access Management

I sit at the table outside Panera Bread in mid-September, expensive coffee, notebook, and pen waiting for use. The sky is a slate pattern of clouds and impending storm. Ten minutes later a man wearing a blue polo shirt with SAM on the chest crosses the parking lot.

"You wouldn't happen to be Matt, would you?"

He sits across from me.

Craig Johnston is the President and CEO of Service Access Management in Berks County. He has a beard the color of fresh snow and face that projects his years of fighting the battle against mental illness and poverty. He is an easy man to speak with and his experience as a therapist shows.

Service Access Management (SAM) was initially part of the Berks County's Mental Health and Mental Retardation office. MHMR assisted with obtaining services for qualified disabled individuals. It split off in July 1997 to become a nonprofit agency with 110 county employees making the switch to the new organization. Since the split, they have become a model for agencies statewide, existing in sixteen counties with a goal of meeting needs without burdening local governments.

"We are a catch-all for people. I like to say that everyone who comes in our doors gets something," Johnston tells me. The main thrust is case management, mobile employees who work throughout the city. "Our office space does not have assigned seats. The case managers have laptops and often work from their cars. They are our feet on the ground."

Referrals are vastly important as calls often come from outside agencies. One of their largest programs is Early Intervention, serving children from birth to age three.

"We'll get calls from neonatal units if they know a baby will have developmental issues," Johnston says. "The BCIU (Berks County Intermediate Unit) has a program that starts at age three. We cover before then and it is one of our heaviest programs in terms of enrollment."

SAM also offers crisis intervention with a team ready to respond every day at any hour to calls that range mental issues to depression and suicidal ideation.

"When the recession was in full swing, our crisis intervention program exploded. We had an influx of calls from new people who had never used our system before," Johnston says. Poverty and mental illness often go hand in hand.

"Imagine being mentally handicapped and now you need to make a living. Not an easy place to be."

There is no set schedule for intakes as they can happen whenever a client walks through the door. Clients will need a clinical diagnosis to obtain services and that presents a unique challenge as the agency will bill and work with medical assistance programs. The intake includes an extensive list of questions to create a holistic picture of needs.

"The Berks County Medicaid Office has been an exceptional partner with us," Johnston says, "they are truly interested in helping those who are in the system."

Even with the help, Johnston faces a familiar issue.

"Like everyone else, our funding has declined. With the drop in funding, we had to execute some layoffs. No direct care positions were cut, but we did lose fifteen staff members with a large amount of experience. What people don't realize is that the clients will suffer over time."

One of SAM's goals is to expand their services and open up the qualifications for access.

"Most of our referrals are word of mouth. The need is far beyond what we can supply, so we tend to keep a low profile. One thing we do is to volunteer at community activities as much as possible to keep ourselves visible. Berks County is our home. We started here and we are aware of that even as we look to expand into additional counties."

With staffing spread thin and a goal of expansion, training becomes a key for success when any employee is in the face of a dangerous situation.

"They are all trained in crisis management techniques. In eighteen years, we've only had one incident of an employee getting hurt," Johnston tells me.

If he had his way, employees would not be needed on the front lines.

"We want clients to be less dependent on the system. They direct their own recovery. Even if we see things we think could help, we can only make suggestions. The recovery must be self-directed."

A balance between a holistic approach to care and patient directed recovery must be maintained.

"We can only stand next to them as they examine their lives and choose to make the right decision. You know how people react when you tell them to do something they aren't ready to do? That's why we keep it patient-focused." Johnston sips from his coffee.

SAM is currently working with Clarion University to set up a measurement for individuals using their services. This will yield important results that can be presented to the decision makers in government. Additional funding, Johnston believes, will follow.

"We really look at community tenure. Are they in a group home? Inpatient hospital? Transitional care? We want them able to live independent of these services and be successful. Human services can be a black hole in a complex and interconnected system." He mentions seeing repeated clients, sometimes within the same month.

As we end our interview, the wind kicks up.

"You know what case management is?" Johnston asks me with a smile, "life coaching. We all could use some life coaching, I think."

Service Access Management

19 North 6th Street

Reading, Pennsylvania 19601

610-236-0530

www.sam-inc.org

Chapter 7

Berks County Community Foundation

The building faces the center of the city on the corner of Court Street, a windowed front with the logo of the Berks County Community Foundation showing to the daily flow of traffic. It is located next to a church and across from the IMAX movie theatre with a parking lot big enough to fit employees and one of church's busses. I enter into a spacious lobby with art fixtures and modern furniture. The receptionist, Lori, ushers me to the meeting room.

I take a seat across from a piece of art the size of my couch at home.

In minutes Kevin Murphy, President of the Community Foundation and Jason Brudereck, Director of Communications, enter the room. Murphy has the presence of an executive; calm, collected, and in control. I compliment the building and he tells me it is the first certified green structure in the city. They capture rain water on the roof and use it to flush the toilets, covering 80% of the water usage in a normal office building.

The foundation manages $60 million in assets and had distributed $2 million in grants last year. In Reading, as nonprofits fight for a single pot of money, the Community Foundation is a key resource. They are contacted numerous times throughout the year as new organizations pop up.

"You would found the nonprofit and establish a board," as Murphy describes the process, "someone on that board, legal counsel or otherwise, has heard of us. You would then either come here to apply for a grant or, less often, we do site visits to your location."

The 2008 recession impacted the foundation as it did every part of the nation.

"We moved from grant making to being a lifeline keeping these businesses up and running. We have, since then, been able to go back towards our regular operation of making grants and meeting needs." Murphy speaks with pride in the accomplishments. "The majority of my job is making connections, 'Oh you have this need? Here's a grant that can meet your needs'."

Murphy has years of experience in the world of community foundations. He has contacts throughout the east coast and networks with cities from Philadelphia to New York and Harrisburg.

"There's a current administration in the city making strides in terms of policy and focus. We need to revitalize Penn Street and downtown. Look across the country, from Times Square in New York to the Avenue of the Arts in Philadelphia, cities have recovered with a focus on their downtown areas." This focus brings in businesses and draws residents from outside the city. "We need young people willing to move away from the suburbs and back to the urban areas."

The salvation of the city lies not in outside help, but in Berks County itself.

"You look at the twenty largest local businesses in the area, all ones with a history. Sixteen of the twenty were founded here. We have this fascination with big business, but small businesses are the key. This means we must rethink investment."

Where nonprofits are focused on holistically treating the individual, Murphy's aim is treating the community and surrounding area. This includes offering complete healthcare and education services at places like Berks Community Health Center, the first nonprofit, federally qualified center in the city. If these services are not available, people will leave and take their commerce with them.

"There are problems with the idea of data surrounding poverty. You can't nail down proof for conflicts that are unresolvable. A lot of times, numbers are picked so they can be moved."

The Community Foundation has received grant applications not connected to the bigger picture of the fight against poverty. "Say you apply for a reading program for schools to improve the level of fifth graders. We'll get data showing a certain anticipated increase of twenty percent. So? They need to tie it into the big picture and show how that improves the city."

It is impossible to track all data surrounding people within the homeless population and lifestyle choices can fall under the radar when being assessed in applications or chances for outside funding.

"We always ask ourselves a common sense question, will this grant hurt anyone?" Murphy does his homework with every application that goes through the process.

"I want the future to be less about grants and more about regional unity."

Murphy tells me he was in Philadelphia yesterday, meeting community foundation leaders in the city and that there are discussions about a metro line running from the Lehigh Valley to Manhattan. "We are close to Philadelphia and New York. What can we learn from each other? What kinds of resources are available? I'd also bring in companies willing to hire city residents. We need to attract businesses here and fully deliver healthcare to the population. Right now you can never supply the entire healthcare you need in Berks County."

I mention a constant refrain from prior conversations, the idea that organizations "don't get any funding."

His eyes widen.

"Don't get any funding? What does that mean? Here's the thing in the nonprofit world, there's a saying that you take on the personality of the group you service. There's a culture of institutional poverty and victimhood. You mean, you don't pay your employees? That's not a way to operate. Most of the time, when a group says they don't get funding, it means they haven't asked."

Murphy shifts to education, a hot topic with public perception of Reading School District as failing.

"I wish people knew that we were all in this together. All the kids out there are ours, it doesn't matter where they were born, who their parents are, or where they live." Social justice and the economic reality go hand in hand. "These kids aren't helped by an education system that is in a freefall of failure. There is no reason you can live on one side of Wyomissing Boulevard and your district spends $12,000 per student and on the other side, they spend $7,000.

Spending should not be hooked on location. The General Assembly is not doing their job. Whose idea was it to put all the poor people in one spot in an urban area? And then give them the chance to tax themselves severely to make it work? We need to level the playing field for all children."

As cogs in the wheel rolling against poverty, every organization must consider their purpose and do so beyond lip service. Do they want to eventually not be needed or do they want to keep going as a viable business?

"We ask every applicant that exact question. Are they seeking to go out of business or stay in business for perpetuity? I mean, if you're an art museum it is easy, we'll just display art forever. If you are a service agency, that's a different story. We can certainly do better. Some problems are not solvable, though."

He mentions the movement in the late 1970's to end the institutional housing options for mentally handicapped individuals. "Not everything can be eradicated like polio. Take domestic violence service providers, for example, domestic violence can be treated but can it every really be eradicated? Look at the Coalition to End Homelessness. Can it ever be eliminated? How does that goal look for them?"

We talk about the Coalition's efforts to find housing for homeless families.

"It is an admirable project. Homelessness is not always from deep poverty. There are plenty of lower middle class families that are one paycheck away from homelessness. You have the addicts and mentally ill on the other side." Both of these groups present unique challenges for the service agencies in the city.

Murphy is a dynamic personality with a long-reaching vision that is needed to fight poverty in Berks County. From his office, with rain water collection on the roof, he plans for the future of Reading's development.

"The new poverty numbers come out this week," Murphy says, "I'm looking forward to it." They are his battle ground, his inspiration, and the Community Foundation will do whatever possible to win the war, one grant application at a time.

Berks County Community Foundation

237 Court Street

Reading, PA 19601

610-685-2223

http://bccf.org

Chapter 8

United Community Services

The first thing that strikes a visitor is the massive vacant lot across from the building. You'll find them all over cities like this, ones dealing with the flight of industry. It is north of Penn Avenue and overlooks Carpenter Technologies, one of the remaining major companies in the city. In a building across the street, shared with a bank, United Community Services is setting up its new location. I enter and get halfway down a flight of stairs before a woman stops me.

She calls me back to the lobby and into their new office space. The room is a jumble of boxes, desks, files, and supplies. I sign the log and Ashley Chambers, Director of Programs, appears from her office at the end of the room. She takes me back through the space and down the initial stairs I had started to descend when I arrived.

A poster hangs on the wall at the bottom of the staircase. It is a collage of students smiling in various work uniforms. Their names and graduation dates are under the pictures.

"These are some of our success stories," Chambers beams, "at least the ones who don't forget to send us pictures."

We keep going to the bottom floor. Another series of class pictures hang on the wall. The usual "class picture" in a yearbook contains uncomfortable smiles and the occasional kid doing something for a laugh. These are different. Each student shows their excitement as the programs at United Community Services succeed in changing their lives.

Groups of students rotate every six months. United Community Services is working on rolling enrollment but, at the moment, it is not an option. Even with this information public, the phones continue to ring.

"All the time," Chambers says, "we'll have kids bring their friends more than once a week. We'd love to have them all in but it's not an option between enrollment periods." UCS started in 2004 with a program for students concurrently working and in school. Four hundred students enrolled and the program had a 99% graduation rate. The focus shifted to students out of school due to dropping out or other circumstances. Individuals are given apprenticeship training in construction and, soon to come, healthcare. They train for job interviews and life skills, including the mayor of Reading running mock interviews.

"If they can survive an interview with the mayor, they can do anything," Chambers tells me. "We work on contacts in the construction industry and other fields and we will make any calls we need to get people working."

There are two teachers on staff, but each staff member is expected to take part in molding the kids. Chambers guides me down a hallway with conference rooms and classrooms. A group of students sit around a circular table in deep discussion. They are part of the current class of fifteen. The organization has relied on money from a Department of Labor grant that is not always a sure thing as it was denied this year.

"The program will look different next year while we apply again and attempt to get approved," Chambers says.

Community service is a major part of the process and students are required ten hours of it to graduate. This can be anything from planting gardens to working with residents at the food pantry that operates on the last Wednesday of every month. The students will often be on the streets talking about United Community Services to their friends, family, and other residents of the city.

This creates a need for expansion on all fronts.

If they could afford it, there would be more staff, teachers, and space. I ask about transportation, as this new building is distance for anyone needing to walk from the center of the city. Chambers tells me that public transportation is one option and, often, they will go the extra mile for students in need.

"We've had homeless students and made calls every day to make sure they had a place to go for the night."

Building trust is a key.

There is an orientation program called Mental Toughness, where each new student is evaluated for their fit. The work is strenuous and, if they fail, they are out. Current students often offer advice to friends wanting to enter the program.

"If one tells me they can't wake up in time to get here at 8:30, then why bother? I'll tell them this isn't their best option." Chambers and her staff know that students must go home and deal with outside forces at night. They teach students ways to identify and overcome these negative forces to find and lead a better life.

Gainful employment is a major step to supporting themselves and their families.

United Community Services also works with the Department of Labor in Pennsylvania as a member of the emergency response team to handle mass corporate layoffs. The team hasn't been activated recently but, if needed, they will respond to a jobsite to educate and assist workers with finding new employment.

The goal is to be the central point for the community to handle issues and assist with overcoming barriers to successful living.

"We had a young man, who just celebrated his one year anniversary from graduation, call us this week. He's working construction, living in his own housing, and supporting his family. He told us it wouldn't have been possible without his time here," Chambers says.

We finish our conversation back in the office space and outside an afternoon slowly moves to dusk. The majority of the students are on a field trip for a service opportunity and the room is quiet.

Employment is a prime force in the recovery of Reading, for what is more of a direct assault on poverty than obtaining a steady job? How many kids would be off the streets if they had a place to work at night? How many students drop out of school and find themselves lost?

With the offerings here, United Community Services could be ten times the size and fill seats in every available classroom. They could have rolling enrollment, online courses, and multiple staff members. They could expand their reach into the city and teach valuable trades to those who need them the most.

Yet, their grant application is denied.

Chambers and her staff will continue to fight, to teach students and rejoice at their success. They will do this all from donations until they can reapply next year.

"We'll be there," Chambers says, "until the day we don't need to exist, if that ever happens."

United Community Services

251 North Front Street

Reading, Pennsylvania 19601

610-374-3319

www.ucsfw.org

Chapter 9

Service Access Management Site Visit

The home office for Service Access Management is a red building of five floors, sitting across from the Berks County Court House. The building, which SAM owns, contains a number of businesses including a bank and more than one law practice. They lease out space and signs are posted all around the structure advertising open spaces. After passing through a security guard and metal detector, I make my way to the third floor.

This elevator ride would be the start of a journey for clients on their path of assistance and life choices.

The elevator stops and the doors open to a waiting room with blue, plastic chairs and white walls.

The waiting room had a distinctly governmental feel. Chairs are connected, magazines strewn in corners and informational posters on billboards attached to the wall. The window for the receptionists is connected with the window for Treatment Access and Services Center (TASC), a service agency sharing space on the same floor.

A handful of people manage to look busy and impatient at the same time.

The waiting room is low key this morning. I had been inside the crowded County Assistance Office, the location where residents applied for Medical Assistance and other programs, before and this is almost serene compared to that chaos. After a few minutes, Robin Teitelbaum appears and we ride the elevator again to the highest floor.

Teitelbaum is the Director of Berks County Operations. She started in the beginning, back in 1987, as a case manager and worked her way up the organizational ladder. She radiates warmth that must have made her a great case manager in her days on the street. We pass an open office space, tables and rows of desks with hookups for laptop chargers, and end up at her office. At the moment, the room is empty as the mobile case managers only meet when necessary.

The focus is to keep them on the street as they cover all of Berks County and work out of their cars.

"We wanted our offices to be accessible to the inner city," Teitelbaum says, "now our accommodations could be better, I mean our doors don't have automatic opening, but we have security guards who help out whenever they can." The empty desks are symbolic of a balance between mobile management and open access. The organization includes a crisis team that is available all hours of the day and night. Staff must be ready to respond when called.

This can get ugly when the calls come from the police.

"We've had to send some crisis team members into rough situations," Teitelbaum tells me. "To work here, you need a release. You do end up taking your job home and that can be stressful. We want our staff to have boundaries and balance."

A specific amount of billable hours is required in a week. If the hours are met before the end of a traditional day, the case manager is free to be done.

"If there's a meeting at school at seven in the morning, they'll have to be there. If a client has a meeting in the evening, they need to find a way to make it work." In a challenging field, this extended schedule is an additional hill to climb for workers trying to make a difference. "We do weekly coaching sessions with staff and supervisors and we encourage communication. We want to know if they are stressed and to be able to help them out."

For Teitelbaum, one of the originals, turnover is concerning. The case managers do not have geographically assigned caseloads. That can lead to miles and time on the road and, even then, not every referral is from a distance. They'll get recommendations from Berks County Prison, outside agencies, and even individuals who cross the street from the courthouse with orders from judges to use their services.

"Our client's voluntarily use our services so, even with court orders, that doesn't necessarily help. We can't force them to go through the program. Some clients have burned bridges at every service agency and hospital in the area. It creates tough situations."

The client volume always outweighs the available services. Between three programs, SAM has roughly 1,500 clients. The Early Intervention program (birth to age 3) gets a hundred referrals a month. Even with this need, over the last three years, governmental funding for mental health services has been cut. The cuts trickle down from counties to providers. Every level feels the pinch.

"It is a challenge to measure success. Is it goals? Recovery? Getting out of the program? What value are employees getting back from their experiences?" Teitelbaum states a frequent chorus in the world of social services.

The government wants quantifiable success. How do you measure it with a population facing a myriad of problems including poverty, mental illness, and addiction?

One of the focus points is working with housing. Lorena Keeley joins our conversation mid-meeting. Keeley oversees SAM's efforts in the housing arena, managing a large grant to provide assisted living services to clients.

"Because the grant is privately funded, we can do much more than an agency only using government money," Keeley tells me. "Clients have a desire for independent living but face a financial barrier to make it happen."

There is an application process with a waiting list. Individuals are considered based on age, mental health diagnosis, income, and other factors. There are four open enrollment periods that coincide with the change in seasons.

After applicants are accepted, they must go through a screening program. Rental units are examined and validated as to being genuine and up to code. Lease agreements are between clients and landlords, with assistance money (Section 8 vouchers) being paid directly to the landlords. Help is also available with gas, electric, and oil bills.

"I just got off a call with Met-Ed," Keeley says, "We received notice of a $5,000 electric bill for a client. We try to negotiate as much as possible for reasonable payment arrangements."

Another unique factor of the housing end is that clients do not have to be open cases within Service Access Management. That ups availability and need throughout the city. A mental health diagnosis is considered valid within a calendar year.

Keeley tells me of a new initiative in the form of a Shelter plus Care program. Individuals must be homeless (defined as living in a place not fit for habitation like a car, under a bridge, or tent) or living in a shelter. The program will provide Section 8 vouchers and requires clients to receive active levels of care and services.

The push is two-fold: you can get help with housing as long as you get help with yourself.

"We must show, yearly, that care dollars spent are equivalent to housing support money." These clients must be open with SAM or another agency to qualify. Keeley also oversees the HMIS database that attempts to log and quantify homeless individuals. These agencies must consistently prove their worth as they chase funding.

It is a tiring, and unending, cycle.

"We are just starting to have the conversation about Code Blue," Keeley tells me. "Our Code Blue is different from other major cities. We don't force people off the street but, if they present to a shelter, they must be accepted even if that means a sleeping bag on the floor."

The sky outside the office is visible through the windows and thick, dark clouds settle over the city. Service Access Management and its employees fight a daily battle to make a difference and both Keeley and Teitelbaum tell me that funding is always an issue.

The demand never ends. The wait-lists keep growing.

Each new program fills and the race is on for more money and resources.

As I walk back to my car, trash and leaves are kicked down the sidewalk with the breeze from an incoming storm. Winter will arrive soon and time is of the essence. The need to provide housing resources is immediate before temperatures drop and every night brings a new sense of dread for those on the street and those working to provide life-saving help.

Chapter 10

Hope Rescue Mission Meeting

After my visit at SAM, I drive north on 6th street until I reach Hope Rescue Mission. Guys amble around the entrance. The sky is still dark and the wind ruffles the trees that flank the building, the white cross hanging bright above the entrance. Hope exists in contrasts, once a sign of wealth with the Reading Railroad and now a sign of wealth and recovery for the spirit. I climb the stairs and meet Pastor Steve Olivo, chaplain for the Mission, inside.

Olivo is tall and thin, voice still carrying traces of the streets of the Brooklyn he called home for many years. He has a presence, an aura that draws an audience. The roots of that would become clear later in the afternoon. For the moment, there was work to do.

We meet in the classroom that holds an office shared by Olivo and Frank Grill. Grill, the Assistant Director who had shown me around the building on my first visit, is out of town for a wedding.

Five residents join us in the room and we start talking.

Hope has a yearly banquet, in mid-October, attended by nearly three hundred people. They are the supporters and a vital lifeline as it does not receive any government funding. Five men at the mission are slated to provide testimonies at the dinner. Robert Turchi, the director, had emailed me and asked if I would help the guys get their stories together. I gladly agreed.

I sit across from Mike, head of the woodshop. He would be interviewed, on stage, by his mentor with a five-minute slot of time. Here was a guy who had faced the heights and depths of life. He had lived here for over a year now and would need to tell his story. As writers, the idea of telling a story comes naturally. For a man rediscovering his life, it can be much harder.

He shifts in his seat.

Mike had acquired everything we associate with success. He owned his own business and lived in a house with his family. Then, like many of the men fighting poverty, addiction latched on and he ended up in Berks County Prison. Hope was his destination mandated by the prison system after his release.

Outside sources often see the poor as consistent, that they are people stuck in years of a pattern. This is not always true. Mike had never experienced homelessness before his addiction and legal issues.

On his first day at Hope, Mike was approached about the woodshop. The staff did not know he had a talent with restoring furniture, that woodworking was his business before everything fell apart. He jumped at the chance. Now he leads the shop, having turned down other job offers for more money to stay and help out. He was also one of the original members of the Mentorship Program, a relationship key to his development and success.

We practice a list of five questions and, finally, it seems his nerves have settled. Mike has found himself refined and refinished, a work in constant progress. We shake hands and he heads back to the daily life of the Mission.

The room empties leaving me with Pastor Olivo. As the afternoon fades, he tells me his story.

Olivo has spent thirty-five years as a clergy member. He found salvation at age twenty-one, and worked on the streets of Brooklyn with David Wilkerson's ministry. He would take students around the streets to show them the realities of life.

"I was saved like Paul," Olivo says, "God knocked me right off my horse. I looked up and said, 'Tell me what you want me to do.'"

He's made a career of front line ministry, working in various outreach organizations. He heads a group that specifically handles sex offenders struggling with poverty and their addiction.

"These guys, they want to hear the truth. They want to know there is a penalty for sin. We don't sugar-coat anything. I meet them and look in their eyes and see the weight of what they've done."

Often homelessness and crime go together. Olivo has ministered to many guys who have committed serious crimes. He speaks in the measured tones of a man fighting daily against the darkness.

"We need to always be ready."

One of the guys in our meeting wants to freestyle his testimony. Olivo is against this and, as anyone who has spoken in public knows, it can be a recipe for disaster. He mentions how Bible College helped him prepare for the experience.

"One night I'm playing basketball downstairs here with my son. A guy comes down and says, 'Steve, can you come upstairs?' I tell him I'll be a few minutes. I keep playing and God says to go upstairs now, so I go. The chapel speaker for the night had not shown up. They asked me if I'd be willing to speak. I talked for fifteen minutes, soaking wet in basketball clothes. Fourteen guys were saved that night."

The chapel services regularly get between one and two hundred men. Olivo runs discipleship classes that are a requirement for the residents. His heart is to see the guys succeed, to have them out on their own in the world making a difference.

"Have you heard about our choir?" he asks. I tell him I haven't.

"God told me he wanted a choir of these men and I went to put it together. It's called Voices of Triumph. I still tear up when I hear them sing. It is twelve guys right now. They are trophies in the hands of God."

Olivo thanks me for writing this book, a huge compliment coming from a lifetime fighter working to change this city one life at a time.

"Any guy here, they all have stories. They're plenty of books to be written just in these walls," he says.

They All Have Stories

The word *poverty* generates a concept and image. Do a quick search on your smartphone and you'll get pictures of individuals on the street looking disheveled and broken. You'll find images of men and women holding signs asking for money and standing in the midst of intersections. They are ones we see and roll up the windows, lock the doors, or punch the gas a little harder to make the yellow light.

We see those struggling as *out there* in a vacuum beyond our sphere of influence.

I had no idea what to expect walking through the doors of Hope Rescue Mission. Dealing with the poor and struggling automatically makes one wonder about their own safety.

I mean, *don't they all just want money?*

The men I met shattered that generalization. The line between a job, family, and house and Hope is not as thick as it seems. These were guys with their own businesses at one point, working forty-hour weeks and pushing through the daily grind.

Poverty comes through the impact of external forces like substance abuse, crime, job loss, or mental illness. In a city with tough economic times, the pull of drugs and alcohol to numb the stress is often too much. When the addiction takes hold, it will ruin lives and land a guy on one of the beds in the lower level of the Mission.

Mercy Pregnancy Center handles the other end of the spectrum, educating a culture about the disadvantages of unexpected pregnancy. Kids change things and Mercy's impact helps to bolster families and provide strength to new mothers and fathers.

Adding a child means an increase in need for food.

These circumstances combined with stressors of existing with limited resources, or without resources altogether, lead people to a breaking point.

The force is a whirlwind that lands clients in the hands of social services and victim support groups like Berks Women in Crisis. The recession of 2008 did nothing to help the situation. The whirlwind grew to a storm and now the city stands in desperate need of support.

This also shows the value of those willing to fight the battle.

The work with those in need is not glamorous and the stories are many. It is a job without a vast salary, with long hours and tragedy on a weekly basis. It is celebrating small victories and mourning over those who lose the fight with their addiction and circumstance. It is done in conversations, prayer, education, laughter and tears.

It is work that will never end.

Because there is always another family to help, another man living on the street, another young mother looking for any assistance she can find, and more children hungry every night. It is a force that drives every level of these service organizations, from the street assistance to the ones gathering food donations and stocking warehouse spaces.

There are still questions to be answered.

How does a city get to the lowest point on the list? Were there any warning signs? Could it be stopped and how does it get better in the future?

Will service agencies ever be more than a band aid over the gushing wounds of societal ills and poverty? Or can there be real and sustainable change?

The future of Reading remains to be written and the battle will continue on a daily basis. The stories are still waiting to be told.

Chapter 11

Reading Redevelopment Authority

As you drive down Penn Street, on any weekday afternoon, you'll find crowds of people. They sit on benches, talk on corners, purchase food from lunch trucks, and pass time. In a city with almost half the residents living at the poverty line, these crowds are reminders of the daily fight to improve the quality of life.

This afternoon I continue past the Santander Bank Arena and turned left on 9th Street. After two blocks, the visage of City Hall looms in the distance. Driving and parking around any city building can be an adventure. It takes two passes to find a garage and a spot on the very top level.

After entry, City Hall spans out in two directions. It is a rectangle with squares inside made up of hallways and offices that house various tenants from the mayor to the city council, police, and fire officials. Walls display informational posters about everything from community activities to public meetings. The city council chamber stands empty, leather-backed chairs and lacquered tables a testament to more than two centuries of political activity.

I make my way to the second floor, getting lost around the offices of the police commissioner and have some questioning glances from employees. Finally, after a few more wrong turns, I stop at the Reading Redevelopment Authority. I open the door to an empty meeting room and second door. I knock on the door and hear a voice beckon me from around the corner.

Adam Mukerji sits behind his desk. Mukerji, in a white Oxford shirt and red tie, is a man used to living within political circles. His hair is closely cropped and he leans back with his hands folded. I mention, offhand, interviewing a representative from Berks Women in Crisis. It is like flipping a switch.

Mukerji starts talking and it takes effort to keep up with my notes.

"Their new building was one of our projects," Mukerji tells me. The goal of the Redevelopment Authority is improving the quality of life in Reading. Though it sounds vague, their efforts are concrete and expansive. They want to bring "walk to work" jobs back to the city. Mukerji doesn't like the term. "No one really walks to work anymore. The jobs just need to be accessible and at a skill set that matches the unemployed worker."

This is harder than it sounds.

Mukerji lists out more recent projects. The company Habasit, operating on a forty acre site of land just outside the city, was the result of a large clean up and rebuild operation. The site had to be thoroughly cleaned of toxic waste. The end result created more than 150 jobs.

Creating and keeping jobs can be a balancing act.

"Quaker Made Meats, you know them?" Mukerji asks me. Their products and distribution network reach well beyond Berks County. "They were going to take their plant outside of the city. I convinced them to stay and we obtained new space for their factory expansion." He talks like a father handling unruly children, high-dollar companies whose ambitions must be met and answered to keep them close. Mukerji is watch dog in a consistent fight to grow and maintain valuable industry. The large arena in the city, formerly the Sovereign Center, was renamed the Santander Arena after the group purchased Sovereign Bank.

"There's a rumor they may want to remove any footprint of their company in Pennsylvania."

"What happens if they leave?" I ask.

"You know what a 'hell or high water' lease is?" he asks me with the tone of a seasoned negotiator, "Santander signed one. Even if they vacate the arena, they will still pay us rent on the property." Mukerji must always stay two steps ahead.

"We have an entire field of dreams here. The main issue is money." The Redevelopment Authority operates on state and federal funds. They get no assistance from the city that reaps results from their efforts. It is a unique political dynamic and the first real glimpse at how deep the arm of politics goes.

A man named Albert Boscov is a major partner and financial backer of the Reading Redevelopment Authority. Boscov is an entrepreneur with multiple department stores bearing his name open in six different states. He has deep pockets and yet maintains an office in the back of the warehouse at Boscov's East, just down the highway from Reading.

Mukerji has nothing but praise for his partner.

"We traveled up and down the coast visiting cities and knew we needed to renovate the arts scene here. There were two big buildings on 2nd Street. With Al's help, we purchased the spaces. It took between $30 and 40$ million dollars to build. In the end, we have one of the best IMAX movie theatres in the surrounding states and the Goggle Works Arts Center," Mukerji tells me. People needed reasons to stay in the city after work and visit the city at night. They are working on adding six family-style restaurants in and around the Arts Section on 2nd Street.

"Have you seen the Goggle Works apartments? They are fifty-nine floors of gorgeous apartments. If I was single, I'd live there. They are like an oasis in the city."

It was not always this way.

Mukerji came to Reading almost fifteen years ago. He was on staff with Governor Christie Whitman in the New Jersey Development Authority, living in New Brunswick with his family.

"We made great strides in New Brunswick while I was there. It was all slums, drug dealers, and X-rated book stores. Now they are building new housing and all those bad elements are gone. Al hand-picked me to come here and I've been here ever since. He's really the biggest benefactor of Reading and a very humble man."

The process of redevelopment, even with financial support, can face resistance.

"We purchased the old American Chain and Cable building on Buttonwood Street. You're talking 198,000 square foot over fourteen acres. Back in the 1970's, all those places used asbestos insulation and lead paint. We were quoted for almost $3 million dollars for cleanup. Word of the asbestos and lead gets out and the newspaper talks to the neighbors."

Local politics in action.

"I decided to hold a town hall meeting. We get the DEP, EPA, local officials, everyone and gather at a church. One lady shows up in camo-fatigues to protest. We talk it out, eventually get approved, and proceed with the demolition and rebuild. That becomes Hydrojet, a company using water to cut pieces of material used in tooling and fabrication."

I ask if the opposition was ever too much or disheartening.

"Never. You need grit, tenacity, and determination. You need to have innovation. They said we'd never build a hotel in the city. We tried six or seven times. Right now we're building a $60 million dollar hotel across from the Santander Arena. It will be open in 2015."

An investment like that creates a number of jobs, a figure that Mukerji produces instantly.

"Around 130. We were promised more conventions with this hotel. Right now, say Disney on Ice comes in. They bring ten trailers of equipment and they all stay out in Wyomissing. There's no reason for that with this hotel. They can stay right next to the arena. The hotel will have a ballroom that can fit 1500 people and have a 950 car garage attached."

The plan is to add value on multiple fronts.

"It will be an anchor for Penn street. We'll add two restaurants to the property. A good hotel always brings in good retail to follow."

The Redevelopment Authority also pushes into rough areas of the city. They are always looking for opportunities to improve the surrounding communities, recently converting a property in the 6th Ward of the city, the highest in crime, poverty, and slums. The pollution was bad enough that it required appearances in Washington, D.C. to get federal approval for construction. The building now houses Sun Rich Foods, a distributor of produce to area businesses.

"Albert flew us down to Washington when we needed to go. We'd get a call in the morning about a meeting that afternoon, and we'd fly down." Mukerji is a man who will do what it takes to finish a project.

"Deals are made on the road, not behind a desk."

The deals don't always pan out and Mukerji tells me that there is always a provision against failure in the lease agreements. If a business doesn't use the property for their stated purpose, it returns to the possession of the Redevelopment Authority.

Their latest purchase is a fifty-acre plot of ground formally owned by Dana Manufacturing. It is prime industrial land and Mukerji is thrilled at the prospects and opportunity.

"When I first started, I had to show I would do what I promised. One of the first projects was the city garage at 6th and Spring Street. I visited the manager's office and I was holding an umbrella inside with all the water leaking from the ceiling. I promised them a new garage and they didn't believe me. Go by there now and check it out. It's a beautiful building."

He has a long list of successes including grants for the Opportunity House homeless shelter, YMCA, Berks Women in Crisis, and the Reading Main Library on 5th Street. My original connecting source to Mukerji came from Kevin Murphy, president of the Community Foundation. Mukerji speaks highly of his colleague. The efforts of the Redevelopment Authority and the Community Foundation are similar on the surface.

"So what is the difference between the Redevelopment Authority and the Community Foundation?" I ask.

"You see their building? Beautiful isn't it? It's a green building, gardens on the roof, beautiful construction. The Community Foundation has endowments. Kevin is sitting on a huge amount of money. Check out my desk. I have a brick under the leg to make it level. We don't get any endowments. The Community Foundation has an austerity budget. It makes things a little easier. I'm always chasing money." He laughs.

We dig deeper.

"You know there's somewhere between 1500 and 2000 abandoned homes here? We're working to get them fixed up and families in with assisted living funds. We work with Habitat for Humanity and after the families put in 400 hours of construction, they can move in the renovated houses. Honestly, I'll work with anyone who has good ideas."

The biggest obstacles to success haven't vanished with recent economic struggles and Mukerji pinpoints two.

"Money and politics. We have a mayor's office with great ideas clashing against a city council that is not supportive." In the interview with Murphy, he mentioned Reading School District being a problem. Mukerji shares that opinion.

"Reading School District is in shambles. We have 68% of the city's population without a GED. We must work with what we have. Look at Google. Who do you think they hire? We're not talking regular people. They want Ph. D's. They want skilled laborers. We don't have an education system producing these kinds of results. This is why you won't see Apple building a plant in Berks County any time soon." Mukerji wants to meet the community on even terms.

"We need to work with the strengths of the community. I've said to numerous people to open up the river." You cross a bridge over the Schuylkill River to enter the city. "Have a community day on the river. Bring in companies that make kayaks and canoes. Do something that will unify the communities. Demographics are changing. Traditional sources of money are drying up. This makes solving the problems even harder."

Planners have thrown around talks to reopen a rail line between Manhattan and Reading.

"The damn tracks are already in the ground. There's no reason not to have it. Think of the map. We are two hours from Baltimore, two and a half hours from New York, and an hour from Philly. Think of the number of people in that corridor alone. There should be a line between Reading and Philly also. You do that and Reading will become a bedroom community for Philadelphia. Look at Hoboken, New Jersey. Property values jumped when the Wall

Street guys started buying houses and taking the train into New York to work. That kind of growth can happen here."

Accountability is another hot button topic in dealing with poor and homeless.

"We must always know our audience and always be there for them," Mukerji says, "nothing gets done without their buying in. Redevelopment is a product. Think of what we have here, the beauty of the area, the wine trails and mushroom exporters. How do we facilitate these strengths?"

We must learn from all the cultures that inform life in the city of Reading.

"My wife says we are not a melting pot. We are a salad. I asked her to explain it. She said the melting pot removes all individuality from the cheeses that are thrown together. With a salad, the individual qualities remain, are easily identified, and still are part of the community."

Mukerji's drive and attitude is contagious and not easily discouraged.

"I've experienced thirteen years of progress since I started. We built the first luxury apartments in the city in fifteen years. The Goggle Works Arts Center gets four million visitors a year. The wine trails are getting more popular. Do you know we have one of the highest concentrations of equestrians in the country? We are still moving forward with that drive and tenacity we need."

He asks if I've ever visited Reading Terminal Market in Philadelphia.

"You know what makes Reading Terminal Market unique? They have a huge array of food choices, all fresh and ready for consumers. There's no reason we can't have the same thing here. We just purchased the old Penn Optical building on south 8th Street. I'm slowly convincing Reading Hospital to partner with us on this as a Community Health Initiative. When the community sees the hospital out and involved, they will turn to them for all their healthcare needs. It is a win for all."

I thank Mukerji for his time. He tells me that I'm lucky. He was to have a meeting but the individual never showed, allowing me more time.

"Reading is the hole in the great donut of development in Berks County. You know what I mean by that? Development is springing up all around us and, here in the middle, we sit with the challenges."

Chapter 12

Redesign Reading

No matter how far I walk, turning corners and passing offices multiple times, I can't find Brian Kelly's location. Kelly is the sole paid employee of Redesign Reading, an organization funded by different city authorities with the goal of social and systematic change. Adam Mukerji suggested I find Kelly and speak with him.

I enter Mayor Vaughn Spencer's office as a last resort. I ask his secretary where I can find Kelly. She tells me to wait a moment and disappears around the corner next to her desk. She returns to say he will be with me soon and that I should have a seat. I wait a few minutes and he appears.

He is taller than I expected, with long hair and the start of a beard. He says he has yet to eat for the day, even though it is almost four in the afternoon, and asks if I'd join him for some food. We leave City Hall, turn left, and make our way two blocks to an El Salvadorian restaurant. He goes to the counter and orders pupusas in flowing Spanish.

Kelly, a graduate of the Wharton School of Business at Penn, worked in Guatemala for a year doing human rights accompaniment in rural and urban locations. He tells me his Spanish is rusty and he likes to practice whenever possible.

We find a booth, soccer blaring on televisions in the corners of the dining area and music flowing from the kitchen, and start talking about poverty.

One of the first things Kelly mentions is that he's visited my website. He talks about having a Catholic background, moving away from it to a more radical version of liberation theology. His interest, he says, is in a systems change component.

"What does local development mean in a global society?" he asks. The waitress arrives with the pupusas, two thick corn tortillas with a bean and cheese filling. He asks me if I ever had one. I tell him I have not and he cuts a chunk off his own.

"This," he says, "is yours."

Kelly is a facilitator.

"I love running meetings. I love finding untapped energy at different places and bringing it together. I find sources and get them in the same room and say, 'let's talk.'"

He douses his plate in hot sauce. People enter the restaurant and take seats behind us. The music from the kitchen gets turned up to where I have trouble hearing him speak. Kelly is unfazed by this, a man in his element.

"I worked in North Philly before I came here," he tells me, "you think Reading is bad? The local gang termed themselves the 'Beirut Boys,' in homage to the images of bombed out houses in the Middle East that looked just like the rowhomes around the corner. The city had no money vested in rehabilitation of properties. Entire blocks had homes without front walls."

Reading, smaller than Philadelphia, has its own unique set of problems. Philadelphia has also never made the top of the poorest cities in the country. Kelly has spent time on the front lines. He sees Reading as his next great challenge.

"I don't believe in permanence. I have no problem with death. We get so hung up on systems and resources. There's a time to move on from things if they aren't working." There are parts of the establishment in this city that will need to end before the generational flow of poverty stops.

"Economic development is boring. Community development is important. What does it look like to build a community?" Kelly goes to the counter and gets me a set of silverware. I unwrap the fork, stab the pupusa, and eat it. Kelly looks satisfied. He keeps talking as the hot sauce flames on my tongue.

"Reading was blasted by macro-economic shift. So what does that mean? Capital can move in seconds. So how do we provision for the needs of people at a base level? We need to think about economic development without money."

The sentence sits in my head for a moment. Kelly's words pick up pace and inflection.

"All systems are human created. They are filled with anti-poor rhetoric. We need to question the fundamentals of whether or not it will fight poverty. That's why ReDesign Reading is a community development corporation. We're a relatively new creation."

Kelly tries, through his organization, to bring different voices to the table. He says sustainable development usually focuses on the middle class. The poor are left out of the conversation. Kelly believes in a focus shift. Green industry must be developed, co-ops created and the entire banking system reconsidered.

"The culture of the folks I worked with in North Philly often needed a personal connection. I've sat through meetings that didn't start until the attendants could find connections. 'Oh, so your uncle is my brother's mechanic?' After they can agree on a personal connection, we get to work. Not before. My instinct was to dive in and get started, because we had important 'business items' to talk about. That wasn't possible. It was a learning experience."

Kelly finishes his plate of pupusas. His phone has vibrated more than once on the table top. He continues to excuse himself and apologize each time. He's a mix of laid back and focused, energetic and efficient. He answers a text message and looks up at me.

"Working with low-income folks can be sexy for about six months. It can also get ugly and frustrating. People often get stuck in their issues and lack of stability and, no matter how hard you try, it can be a struggle to get them on board. But, let's be clear, this is the same with people of all class backgrounds. Everyone else just has a little more resources. The poor have to weather the storm when things get hard."

Kelly pays the check. The heat from my two small slices of pupusa is now a faint burning.

"There are four kinds of people in the social change movement; the helper, the rebel, the organizer, and the advocate. The trick is figuring out how to help them work together. You can have groups filled with one or two of the same kinds and they won't get anything done."

I ask about the involvement of churches.

"Churches tend to focus on social service delivery, things like supporting felons or pregnancy centers, which is the helper role. That is needed, but not a solution. Non-resident pastors and members can be disconnected from the community. Oh, they'll have 'Community Days.' That's great for a nice time but, in the end, the problems maintain. One role is not better than the others. The important thing for each of us is to decide which of these roles we want to play as change agents in this world."

He checks his phone again.

"We should probably get walking to the Bike Hub."

The Hub is ReDesign Reading's signature project, a bike shop that repurposes bikes and sells them. They hold classes for neighborhood kids to teach bike building skills. We leave the restaurant and head towards the Santander Arena. The sun is making its way down and a steady breeze presses against our faces as we walk.

"The key to social change is grassroots mobilization. When force is strong enough, it pressures the system to bend towards it. Look at the Civil Rights Movement. The force causes a new framing of the conversation."

The conversation, in his view, must be reframed.

"Often times the combination of incentives that exist make no sense to poor people. If you have an unmarried couple, in a stable relationship for years living together and collecting benefits, and you tell them to get married, why would they do it? If it means losing assistance with food and money, there's no reason. The incentives don't match the goals."

People with less financial latitude are blamed more for the problems.

"There are three levels of poverty. The abject poor have no resources, income, or prospects. The working poor are trying, but the numbers don't work in their favor. The income insecure are almost half of the population. If one member of the family loses income, the entire family will be on the street within six months."

He provides an illustration that hits home.

"Look at the business world. There's a huge pay difference between executives and low-level employees. Say one is off for a day or an extended period of time. Who is noticed more? The executive is out and no one notices because the company picks up the slack. You lose the front desk person, the security guard, the base level employee, and it impacts everyone. The base employee is more important and the pay difference between the two is huge."

Kelly's Community Development Corporation is focused on the working poor. He wants to improve the quality of life and sees it as more important than jobs. The problem is the conflict between economic and social issues. Look at the social system. We take the 'bad' people out and put new people in their place. It's why there are overcrowded prisons.

Kelly and I almost get hit by a car turning in front of us in the crosswalk.

"I love finding untapped potential and underutilized resources and bringing them together. My goal is to create hope and put good people in a positive project. Our Bike Hub brings people together across classes. We get executives and unemployed people riding together, looking across their bikes and having conversation. It is a cross-class experiment."

We start the final block to the Bike Hub. I try to mentally track my progress as Kelly is staying at the Hub and I'll need to return to my car.

"We want to redefine volunteering and sweat equity. Say you volunteer for twenty hours a week. How can you get paid? How about singing lessons for your kid? How about food from a sustainable garden or local farm? How about having your rent paid for your volunteerism?"

He would love to create a Community Land Trust model in Reading.

We enter the Bike Hub. Three kids wait on an old couch for the lesson to start. I meet Anthony, the volunteer running the desk. Bikes fill the room. A handful of other kids arrive. Kelly checks his phone. We have a minute.

"Did you see the community chalk board?" Kelly asks me. I tell him I have not. "It's something we've seen in other cities, and a group of young folks got together to launch here in Reading. We set up a chalk board with the phrase, 'I love Reading because…' People come along and fill in whatever they want. We take pictures and post them to our website."

Kelly walks me to the door. Class starts as I leave the hub and make my way back to the garage. If there is anyone who may be the key to changing the city, it is this lanky guy with the bike shop and big ideas. We shake hands.

"I believe we can take currency out of the equation," Kelly says as more kids arrive on their bikes and park them outside.

ReDesign Reading CDC

237 Court Street

Reading, Pennsylvania 19601

610-685-2236

www.redesignreading.org

Chapter 13

Thanksgiving at Hope Rescue Mission

The holidays are the time of year that people look towards poverty, naturally inclined to reach out and help their fellow man or woman. This is the point where charities can make their gains as they near the challenges of winter.

Thanksgiving at Hope Rescue Mission is one of the longest-running holiday functions in the city.

An early snowstorm had moved through the night before. We wake up, as a family, and prepare for relatives who were coming over later in the afternoon. After depositing the turkey in the oven, I leave for the Mission and their meal at noon.

This year they are fully staffed with volunteers. The parking lot has no spaces available when I arrive, forcing me to an opening at the strip mall across the street. I climb the stairs in the midst of a small crowd waiting to get inside. Men talk with their families who were there to visit. Girlfriends sit across from guys and hold their hands. Someone plays a guitar in the corner of the lobby.

Robert Turchi, the director of the Mission, crosses the room in my direction. I ask him about the crowd.

"Last year we fed two hundred and fifty people. We're probably looking at the same number this time. We have almost the same number of volunteers. They cooked twenty-five turkeys," he tells me. He stops and greets people more than once in our brief conversation, an important player in the effort to make the holiday feel like home to men who hadn't crossed the threshold in years.

The doors to the dining area open and a line forms, allowing people to file inside. I slip in step with the others and enter the large dining space. Tables are made and places set. Volunteers stand along the wall, hands gloved and ready, watching those who enter with me. I find room and squeeze in between two groups.

Pastor Steve Olivo, the chaplain of the Mission, offers a short message about God touching his life. He mentions Jesus telling his followers, "When you give a cup of water to someone in need, you do it to me." He finishes his word asks for Christian Leinbach to speak.

Leinbach, wearing a blue dress shirt and khakis, is the head Berks County Commissioner. He has the presence of a government official and his voice easily projects across the room. He prays, head of silver hair lowered, and offers up a mix of thanks for the food and friends and wishes for salvation for those who did not yet know their creator.

The action starts in a flurry of movement. Volunteers young and old cover each table, providing plates of food. I make the rounds to talk with Olivo and Frank Grill, the associate director of the Mission. I ask Grill about their banquet that occurred last month.

"Last year, at our banquet, we cleared about $6,000 dollars," Grill said, "this year we opened things up to corporate sponsorship for the first time in the history of the Mission. We had a planned giving program around the number 120, as this is our 120th year in existence and it costs roughly $120 dollars to feed, house, and clothe a guy for a week. These moves together had surprising success."

A volunteer interrupts to ask Grill about finding extra water. He leaves me for a moment and returns.

"We had an individual at the banquet offer to match the first $4,000 dollars we received. The corporations really stepped up. We ended up clearing $30,000 dollars, more than we had ever done before."

A second volunteer appears stating that a man outside in a wheelchair wants to join the meal but cannot as the building is not handicap accessible. Grill tells the volunteer to prepare a plate and that they will deliver it to the guy's house, the meal itself available to residents and nonresidents of the Mission.

Olivo had told me minutes before that they were up over a hundred residents.

The dining hall easily fills with twice that number.

I ask Grill how he is doing. His face drops for a moment and his expression shifts.

"Satan attacks," he says. An elderly relative was in the midst of an extended ICU stay. His wife and children were dealing with their own sets of health issues. Grill, standing in the hustle of activity, is solemn.

"We've had some things here too. Guys have struggled recently. We had to dismiss some from the discipleship program. The choir lost a section of members." They had a night at the Mission planned in December to show off the choir with a number of holiday songs and skits. Now, Grill says, that night may not happen. "I started here in 2012 and was riding this high. 2014 was almost too busy and we'd had trouble keeping up. Now all this."

He shakes his head

After a few moments the cloud quickly passes. Grill puts on his smile. He pats me on the shoulder and we part ways.

A local news station, Channel 69 WFMZ, arrives to broadcast a report about the meal, the anchor looks uncomfortable in her winter coat and heels. Before I leave, I stop to speak with Commissioner Leinbach.

"Jesus is the solution," he says, "change the man and real change can happen." He hands over a business card. This is the first government official I had met out in the field serving the poor. I head for the door, leaving the noise, conversation, and community behind.

Traffic is light on the drive back home. Val calls to tell me about the turkey being finished. I pull away looking at the Mission in my rear-view mirror. Men still gather at the entrance. Winter has yet to fully arrive and some coldness has crept through the doors. Hope is making a difference and Grill assures me they will find a way through their issues. He says that stories are used in the discipleship classes. The men learn from their fellow men dealing with the same problems and addictions.

"Reading is in a unique position," Leinbach tells me, "as we've been on the top of the poverty list for years." The city has hit bottom and serves as a testing ground, a blank slate for recovery efforts on all levels of society.

Time will tell if it can achieve real and sustainable change.

Chapter 14

Christmas at Mercy Community Crisis Pregnancy Center

As we near Christmas of 2014, I collect donations for Mercy Community Crisis Pregnancy Center. I had emailed Sherry, the director, and received a list of their top five needs. The radiology department at Pottstown Hospital, where my mother works, sponsors Mercy as their charity for Christmas and their donations easily double my own.

On a frigid Thursday in December, I leave work early and make my way across the city.

I had two interviews scheduled in the afternoon, both follow-ups at City Hall. In the hours before leaving, both had contacted me to reschedule. Tis the season, I thought, as I emailed Sherry and asked her if I could stay some extra time. She readily agreed.

I park around the corner from Mercy and take three trips to unload my car. When I finish, Sherry introduces me to a young woman working the desk, saying her name is Casey and she would love to do an interview.

We sit down and she narrows her eyes at me.

"Did you work at Pottstown Hospital?" she asks. I affirm her suspicion. "I was there as a scheduler in the business office," she replies. The hospital had recently cut the entire business office and condensed it with another hospital in their network.

"Sherry came to my church last spring," Casey says, "She spoke and something inside just clicked. I had thought about volunteering for a while and her words stirred something."

The door opens behind me and a woman enters carrying boxes. She says she has additional donations in her car. I join Casey and Sherry in the unloading process. The front hallway is lined with bags of clothes and boxes of diapers and wipes. They are in the midst of that time of year that people remember charities.

"People think it's scary," Casey tells me, "you're not going to get shot if you drive in here. You don't need your guard up. Honestly, our clients are more fearful and guarded than we are. Sometimes they just need a happy face."

Casey wears many hats during her volunteer hours. She sorts clothes, makes appointments, handles paperwork, and even facilitates peer counseling sessions.

"The biggest thing is; we need to keep everything in perspective. Not everyone is perfect. We can't get sucked in to the dramatics and we need to remember that it's not about us. Our faith is the foundation. When clients come here, they will hear about the Bible and Jesus."

The time crosses over two in the afternoon. Casey mentions there was a counseling session scheduled for that hour.

Fifteen minutes later the clients still have not arrived.

"See, I get worried when we have a no-show," Casey says, "I wonder what prevented her from getting here and if she's okay." Something as simple as a missed meeting can be cause for great concern. Violence and crime, come with the territory for women who attempt to find their way out of dangerous relationships.

We talk about "solutions," a dangerous term in the world of nonprofits and the fight against poverty. Sherry emerges from a back office.

I mention the opinion that there can often be disconnection between the decision makers and the individuals and families utilizing services.

She agrees with me.

"We try to keep in mind the long view. I have a client who is just getting her degree in her late twenties. We've helped her and encouraged her to make positive choices. Now, in the eyes of some, that's not a success. They want numbers and statistics showing concrete results in a short amount of time. That's just not the case."

"We need to attack the problem before it starts," Casey tells us, "Churches should be talking about sex to their teens, and parents should be talking about it. They need to be real and get their hands dirty. It's like saying, 'oh, the water's cold' without jumping in."

The fight is unending and the challenge increases when poverty is in the mix.

"We had a teenage client in here the other week for a pregnancy test," Sherry says, "if it was negative, she wanted information on how to get pregnant, as her mother wanted to be a grandmother. In other situations, clients are just looking for someone to love them. They think a baby will serve that purpose."

"Survival is different for everyone," Casey folds her hands on the desk, "We may think; go from A to B to C, but for them it is just A to B, A to B."

Poverty forces their clients into a short form view of the world. They survive, one day to the next, and keep living.

As I walk back to my car I pass the nail salon. A woman sits inside waiting to get serviced. Two children sit next to her on the seats, looking at me through the window. I consider their ages and both should be in school.

Yet, there they are, looking at the city that will present them two paths, one to a better life and the other to somewhere much darker.

Chapter 15

Mayor Vaughn Spencer

Inside the office of Mayor Vaughn Spencer, his receptionist works on decorations in the lobby area, sifting through a box of ornaments and lights for an artificial tree that sits in the corner. This was a few weeks before the real "city tree" would make international headlines for being an imitation of the *Charlie Brown* version with sparse limbs, spare needles, and a single red ornament.

This morning, the hopes of the holidays still lay before us.

I ask the receptionist if she needs any help and she declines. In a few minutes she tells me to go back to the office. Spencer is one of the main faces of Reading and tackling poverty falls directly into his lap.

He is a tall man with a shaved head, booming voice, and strong handshake. He wears a suit of all black and greets me with a smile. The office, he tells me, is a holdover from the days of the founding fathers and their council government. The suite is spacious, with a full-sized meeting table and connected kitchen.

Spencer, like Adam Mukerji in his interview, speaks with flow and passion and he jumps into a discussion of poverty. He has grown up in Reading and still lives on 12th Street. One of the first things he mentions is City Lights Shelter.

"We need to understand reality and have balance while we meet a need. City Lights is needed and we are working with them to get it open as soon as possible." The shelter had been mentioned before and clearly left a sting with the policymakers involved. In a city with a large homeless population, any efficient shelter properties are valuable and, when City Lights was shut down after coding violations, it left a void that the other organizations like Hope Rescue Mission and Opportunity House had to pick up.

At the moment, Hope is pushing capacity.

The conversation quickly turns to an overview of the problems Spencer has inherited in his first term as Mayor.

"We lost manufacturing jobs. We need to create them and not just jobs, but ones with benefits and salary. The Community Foundation flew us out to Detroit to visit after their collapse. You ever go to Detroit? There are masses of vacant homes, the further you get out of the city." Spencer tells me he has family members in Michigan and, as he relates the story of Detroit's collapse, he seems down, but inspired.

"When a business wants to come into Reading, you know what they do? They ask us what the test scores are in the area for the students. They want to know if they'll have an educated workforce in the city. They want to know the local income base to see if people will have enough money to buy their products. At the moment, we're not in a good spot. They see our results and will they come here?"

The city offers incentives to try and overcome the hurdles. They are pushing things like the Jumpstart Incubator Initiative and the Main Street Initiative. They offer tax incentives for business that, Spencer admits, can leave the city the moment the incentives expire. It creates and contributes to the cycle of flight that is harming Reading's chance to climb out of the depths.

"How do we combat this flight? We need to build up our small businesses. We're working with the local collages to set up a program to train small business owners. We have some new industrial sites coming, places like the Buttonwood Gateway, Penn Optical, and the Canal Street area. We have great diversity here and we need to get small businesses on Main Street. We need to improve parking and lighting."

Reading was once a city that drew visitors on the Penn Street corridor. Families would travel into the city on weekends to shop and visit different attractions. Today, you drive through during the day and see the groups of unemployed and underemployed. Penn Street is alive, but not with the optimism that Spencer desires. The foot traffic is there and, if the right businesses can find homes, they will be successful.

Spencer sees hope for Reading coming from within.

"I went down to the United States Conference of Mayors in Lexington, Kentucky. They had a set up where we could pitch the plans we have for our cities and get feedback. It was a great experience." He takes a breath.

"The 9th Street Corridor will be big for us." The street runs north and south, intersecting with Penn Street's east and west path. It offers an alternative to the business on Penn and a chance to extend the walking and shopping area deeper into the city. It also sits at the corner of the new hotel construction that was the pride of Adam Mukerji's projects.

"We have the 8th and Oley complex, the recording studio purchased at 9th and Douglas, and the potential at the Reading Railroad station. We need to give people a reason to come in and these places are working to provide that reason."

Spencer is proud of his roots.

"We have a great city, a walkable city. We are one of the best biking areas on the east coast. We have so many reasons to bring people in here. We are adding the hotel by the arena, new restaurants and attractions."

Jessica, the Mayor's assistant, enters the office and tells us that a wedding has arrived. They had not shown up that morning and now arrived in the midst of our interview. Spencer apologizes and we agree to follow up in the future.

*

"I got calls from across the country," Spencer tells me. It is the first week of 2015. This afternoon, as I enter the office, three police officers are leaving. The Mayor had just finished a meeting. He laughs about the Christmas tree as we settle back in our positions at the massive meeting table.

The conversation shifts to education.

"Reading School District is not failing the city," Spencer says, "There are a lot of good kids in the system. They are doing good things. The focus is always on the bad kids. Our local news coverage focuses on the bad. Do they talk about the academic achievements? About the colleges the seniors are going to? No. They love to talk about the bad." The educational landscape of the city is changing. Immigration spanning from New York to Puerto Rico has provided classrooms of students dealing with issues like languages.

"Kids are losing their Spanish. International families struggle to develop English skills. Kids with limited language have trouble with tests and assessments. The scores drop and that's what gets published out there." Spencer himself is a graduate of the district. "There used to be families in the city, professionals concerned with their children's education. These families moved out to the suburbs. There are good programs out there though. The United Way is working to get all students in third grade reading at a third grade level."

The schools in Reading are an important link in the chain of the fight against poverty. I had spent a semester observing a classroom in the Citadel, Reading's 9th grade center. The building was a converted hospital and the classroom I was in used to be a part of the morgue. The school had more than one student die that semester in shootings. The negative is always more memorable than the positive and maybe Spencer is right.

The bigger question is what conditions drive crime to that level and how involved is the widespread poverty on the streets.

The temperature drops outside.

"What advice would you give to someone sleeping in their car tonight?" I ask, aiming for a more philosophical direction.

"I'd tell them to find adequate shelter, to get to a safe space. Now, I'd like to tell you the shelters we have in the city are adequate but, they're not. I'm calling a meeting this month with the heads of the outreach programs in the city. We need a plan to triage the current homeless population out there."

This city, with so much need, is not close to being prepared to meet the need. The fight would only get worse before it improved.

"We're working on it. We started the Clean City Initiative to get the graffiti areas cleaned up. You know, we had some record keeping issues here in the past. Our budgets were inaccurate, the tax collection was too low and the rates were off. Now, how do we deal with the deficit? We have two major resources, water or parking, and we may need to monetize one of them."

As much as the blame for poverty and homelessness can be placed on the individuals involved, Reading is dealing with issues from government on down.

Spencer is in the midst of preparing his announcement of running for a second term of office. He has initiatives and plans that were not finished and the desire to see them through. If a leadership change does occur, it could be the death blow to any valuable progress.

"In five years I see us developing a tax base. I see us sharing resources. Some of the surrounding communities still have volunteer fire departments. We have a great fire department in the city and there's no reason we can't look into having substations outside city lines to offer help. Our resources can assist in meeting the needs of our surrounding neighbors. We need unity.

"In ten years, Reading will reinvent itself. Did you see the Philly just announced a bike share program? We are announcing ours within the next month or so. Reading has so many assets here. We are one of the top mountain biking areas in the region. Does that mean adding bike lanes in the city? Then we need to do it and encourage our visitors."

With the current traffic struggles, it would be an ambitious undertaking.

"We can get there. Look at Lancaster." Lancaster is a city not far from Reading, with a more stable economy and infrastructure. "In ten years we can get to that level. It will take time but, it can all happen."

Chapter 16

Glad Tidings Church

Glad Tidings is located about five minutes down the highway from the city of Reading. It has almost surpassed its hundredth birthday and expanded from a small church to a main campus that houses more than two-thousand people over two services every Sunday and a satellite campus in the city of Kutztown. Val and I had driven by the complex for more than a year after we moved to the area and, one Sunday, decided to go in and visit.

Six years later and we call it our home church.

At the start of this project, I had reached out to fifteen churches in the area and received no response. I emailed Glad Tidings and they were happy to set up a meeting for me with Pastor Bryan Koch.

On a late afternoon in January, one that barely cracks the 10 degree mark, I drive to church and park just outside the office.

Koch, head pastor at Glad Tidings, greets me with a warm handshake and smile. He maintains the size and build of the local baseball star that was drafted through the Chicago White Sox system. After a stint in the majors, he was struck by a fastball that blinded his left eye. He found his way into ministry and, twenty-five years later, now stands at the head of one of the largest churches in Berks County.

He ushers me into his office, a room furnished in warm tones and comfortable furniture, and we sit at a circular meeting table. He wears a blue and white dress shirt over a pair of jeans and eases into conversation with the smoothness of an experienced clergyman. Skilled church leaders build relationships and Koch is one of the best.

I mention the lack of response from local churches to the interview emails.

"See, there's the problem," Koch says, "The church should be nonpolitical. There are times we can get caught up in all the personalities and politics involved. Can you imagine what we could get done if we'd all work together?"

Koch knows and understands the local landscape of communities of faith.

"In 2012 we had a strategic planning session. I conducted my own focus group and asked people what was the first thing they thought of when they heard GT. They all said it was the 'big church.' We had to switch the focus. I didn't want us to be known as only the big church. We needed to push the focus onto the community, to mobilize and encourage people."

I ask if there were ever any failed missions or mission opportunities in Koch's experience. He mentions Convoy of Hope, an outreach event that happened in Reading around an economic collapse in 2012.

"Our focus was a partnership across local churches and organizations. We went into the city and really made an impact."

Sherry Camelleri, the director of Mercy Pregnancy Center, had told me about Convoy of Hope and how one of her clients was frustrated with the experience. After Convoy left the city, she had returned to Mercy looking for the same level of assistance. In her view, the churches vanished while the need persisted.

"That woman is correct," Koch acknowledges, "Convoy was never meant to be a permanent fix. It was more to show what we could do if we all banded together. There have been plenty of failed endeavors. If money was the only problem, we'd have it fixed. We need to help the whole person with coordination and support."

At a past church service, one of the associate pastors mentioned a bereavement ministry. Koch takes me through the experience of a person entering it for the first time.

"That process has changed over the years. Initially, we'd run to the office and get a hundred-dollar Giant gift card so they could get food. We'd hand them money and they'd leave to go back to their habits or addictions. We knew that the process needed to expand. Now, people meet with a Power of One counselor. They talk about finances, job opportunities, examine local assistance opportunities, and meet with certified financial counselors. They examine why they'd ended up in the situation in the first place."

"So the process is a holistic effort?" I ask.

"Yes, totally. We give them recommendations towards success, even if that means getting their resume to the appropriate people. We have a lot of money budgeted to the benevolence ministry. Our first goals are that they have food and heat. We need to give tangible help."

Glad Tidings is a large enough church that their yearly budged expands past the $4 million mark. Resources are available to make a difference in the local and national mission fields. With an abundance of need and availability, who makes the final say towards sending out financial, physical, and human resources?

"There's a saying, 'if it is all missions, then none of it is.' The choice is an important one. We look to the Bible for our guidance and ask ourselves where is our Jerusalem? We start local and then go global. People are afraid of Reading but, even so, our first responsibility is here. This is our mission field."

Koch, and Glad Tidings, approaches the mission field with a unique point of view.

"We always partner with local churches and outreaches. It's not about us; it is about what we can do together. There's a mix of need with church planting efforts and continued care. We want to be partners in success. Take the Greybills," Doug and Liz Greybill operate an outreach ministry working with homeless veterans in Reading. They are also members of Glad Tidings. "We just sent a team to their house to help with organizing materials and their storage area. They needed more living space, organization, and ease in getting the materials they need from storage."

The church includes a thriving small group community. More than a hundred groups gather during the week across Berks County. Koch's passion is that no part of the church hesitates to make a difference.

"I believe every small group has a responsibility to the community. They each adopt an outreach or local family to assist. We have Go Groups that meet for prayer and then hit the city to help at places like Hope Rescue Mission. These groups are filled with people not content to just eat brownies, hold hands, and sing."

After almost thirty years of ministry, Koch is not afraid to call his congregation to a higher level of engagement.

"I was meeting with a group of small business owners the other week. I challenged them to consider what they were doing to make the world a better place. I told them, if they aren't thinking about their impact on the community, their businesses can suffer. We all need to ask ourselves how we can make a difference."

Koch pushes on as we discuss agencies like Mercy Pregnancy Center and Hope Rescue Mission.

"Mission is powerful. We've done a study. Eight out of ten people give their first offering to missions. We even send them a thank you note. There is a desire in all of us to help, to really reach the community and be a part of something bigger."

Kevin Murphy, head of the Berks Community Foundation, had mentioned the end result goals of outreach organizations. They had two options that needed to be consideration. Were they built to exist in perpetuity or were they meant to end at some point? It is a question for the church as well.

"We have people in some rough areas of the world, places where entire teams of missionaries get thrown out by a hostile government. It is never our goal to have a missionary enter a field and be there for their entire life. That's not in the Assemblies of God doctrine. We go in to partner with the indigenous church and local leaders. We don't want places dependent on American leadership. The locals need to take ownership."

Koch's passion is unity and partnership. His drive is to move these qualities out into the community. There are people sitting in seats on Sundays thinking that missions are not their problem. There are people more concerned about getting fed than helping others. We are in the midst of a consumer culture and, as part of a large church, Koch fights against the tide.

"You know, most churches don't see their hundredth birthday? The church must make a difference and be in the community. In society, church tends to be more famous for what they can't do than what they accomplish."

He talks about the Crossroads XP program. It is a team of volunteers working in four Reading schools and the Olivet Boys and Girls Clubs. They go into the schools with resources for teachers and students, from food and supplies to character education sessions.

"We are coming to you. There's no offering involved, we're not slamming kids over the head with Jesus. Right now, if we had more manpower, we could get into even more schools. The teachers love it."

Glad Tidings is working to shift the dynamics of modern church. In Koch's opinion, there's still too much of a business influence.

"Churches tend to measure things in nickels and noses. Did we put more money into the offering this week and more noses in the seats? We look at that more than whether or not we are equipping people for service and employing them to do the works of God."

As we talk, Koch shapes a message for those down the road in deep poverty.

"The bottom line is that they know they are needed and can make a difference. Too many people feel like their contributions don't make a difference. They can find a need and fill it. Right now, I want to activate people and push them to the edge." He makes fists and spreads them out wide, the orator kicking in as his volume increases.

"Think of the churches in the area. If we could all capture this vision, what could happen? We need to ask ourselves, are we doing what Jesus did? I want people to know that there is hope beyond their situation. The solution isn't just money."

If Koch could reach every struggling person in Reading and Berks County, he would.

"I thank God for places like Hope Rescue Mission, Family Promise, and Mercy Community Center. There are not outreaches like these everywhere. People need to know that the light at the end of the tunnel isn't always a train. If we all just did our part, we'd see change. We are better together and we need to make sure we celebrate the good things that are happening."

Koch explains his excitement at the unity that can be gained by sharing the stories of the agencies at work to make Reading a better place and, he believes, a shared story can make a real difference. His support and the resources of Glad Tidings are immensely valuable in this fight and will continue through his leadership. The city is their Jerusalem and their domestic efforts will persist until changes are in place and the suffering and struggle can finally end.

Chapter 17

Reading City Councilwoman Donna Reed

"We grew up on a farm out in Muhlenberg that my grandparents bought in 1910. My father told us stories about the poor guys who would walk up our lane during the Depression years when he and his brothers were young. My grandmother would make them dinner and my grandfather told them they could sleep in the barn overnight. The next morning, they would need to move on. They'd see new guys – in those days they were referred to as hobos – nearly every night. One of my dad's most clear, Depression-era memories was his family helping out the poor."

Donna Reed smiled, blue eyes flashing warmth over her pink blazer and sweater. Reed has served on the Reading City Council for more than a decade. She worked for the *Reading Eagle* for 23 years, named the first female op-ed columnist in 1977 a year after being hired. She wears many hats at the moment: serving on Council, working as an editor and reporter at the *Ephrata Review*, as a free-lance writer, and, at some point, completing a biography of the late Sen. Michael A. O'Pake.

She is passionate about the history of Reading and Berks County, proud of her heritage, and connected to the ways in which the past influences the present.

"We had a strong work history here, the Pennsylvania Dutch worked hard for what they had. Somewhere along the way, with the changes in demographics, we lost that reputation. The Pennsylvania Dutch also gave us their judgementalism, for better or worse."

Our talk moves to politics.

"We need politics beyond partisans. We need to watch the charities in the city and what exactly they are doing with their donations. We need more conversation and action. People need incentives, a hand up and not a hand out," Reed says.

Hope Rescue Mission distributes cards with this phrase printed on the back.

One of Reading's main projects at the moment is the hotel going up across from Santander Arena. I ask how a person sleeping on the floor of a homeless shelter should believe the new hotel will improve their condition.

"You need to talk with Craig Poole, the manager of the hotel. He's a man of the people. He's ready to hire the people who need the jobs. The building is connected to those struggling by offering a level of gainful employment. It comes down to what each person is able to do. The hotel is a good start," Reed tells me.

As a member of city government, Reed cares about her constituents. She uses a second phrase that I'd heard before, that Reading is the hole in the donut, surrounding towns unable and often unwilling to help with the problem.

"We all missed the boat," Reed says.

The construction of the hotel is connected with the overall condition of the Penn Street corridor. It took 50 years to get a civic center added to the city on the tail end of a 15-year stalemate that began with an election referendum in 1985. The small stores suffered, many closing their doors. This chain of events, one of many according to Reed, is symptomatic of the often dysfunctional elements of city government and fiscal management.

Political sparring produces economic struggle in its wake.

"You know the business coming into the old Dana site? BioGen Holdings? They said we'd be looking at 200 jobs. It was a $350 million dollar investment that included tax-free bonds and incentives. You know what those jobs were? Construction. In the end, we're left with 55 jobs. $350 million for 55 jobs. Where is the payoff for those who need it?"

The firm eventually decided against locating in the city.

The bottom line is clear.

"Where are the jobs? No jobs are out there for a disadvantaged workforce."

I ask about City Lights Shelter, a much-needed shelter space dealing with the city and a number of code violations. With the current shelters at or over capacity, new space is vital.

"We bent over backwards for them and reopened the place. If you'd seen the pictures from inside, you'd understand. They had exposed electrical wires. It didn't look safe. The problem is no equitable sharing of burden. The suburbs don't want homeless shelters. They'll donate and help out as long as the shelters stay in the urban center. City Lights is now housing people overnight. We also have the YMCA on Sixth Street and the homeless shelter on Second Street. There are crowded shelters and, still, a disgusting segregation exists."

In a city with needs, many charities and economic development entities operate. They exist on different levels of success and influence. This generates competition and economic territory is valuable.

"No one is willing to share any money. There's this attitude of 'don't step on my foot.' I mean, can't we all be Greater Reading? It's like high school and no one has graduated. People identify with their specific territories and not the overall picture," Reed says of both charities and economic development organizations.

The City of Reading is currently in Act 47. Act 47, the Financially Distressed Municipalities Act, allows the Commonwealth of Pennsylvania to declare a city financially distressed. It also allows for the restructuring of debt, limits the ability of government funding, opens the city to participation in federal debt adjustments and bankruptcy, and allows area municipalities to merge to alleviate economic stresses.

For a person so engaged in history, Reed's outlook towards the future is less optimistic than most.

"I think reestablishing the railway to Philadelphia is vitally important," noting the challenges of municipal cooperation along the length of the railroad from Philadelphia to Reading and sufficient federal, state, and local funding.

"The railroad was once the lifeblood of the city, with Reading Railroad being the largest corporation in the country at one point," she said. "Industries that were once the foothold of this city are gone. Will Reading find the new niche to save it? We need more multi-use locations for industry."

Reed, with her history at the *Reading Eagle*, believes that her old employer is missing opportunities in the city.

"The newspaper could do more. They could establish a new brick-and-mortar location in the city, a salon location with media and idea incubation centers. They do some good things but they could do more. You know the buildings around the newspaper offices? Some large spaces stand empty and the paper owns them already. They could open up valuable locations. Have members of the media meet with the community to interact over relevant issues."

Sovereign Bank, a local company, recently removed all their locations from Berks County. Santander moved in. Reed isn't convinced that Santander is invested in the city.

"You should talk to Dick Ehst, a lead guy at Customers Bank. They are local and he has some great things in the works," she said.

Reed wants to break down the long-standing walls between government and the people.

"We need a street-level Chamber of Commerce and Business Bureau. They are hidden away far in fifth-floor offices albeit on Penn Street, in a building with challenging parking and access," she said.

"We need boots on the ground to promote the city. Imagine, government people on the streets talking with everyone, from the homeless to the business people. Suddenly, they are more than names, they are real people."

Reed speaks of a current project working to lower teen pregnancy by 40 percent when we reach 2022. A city mired in the midst of poverty needs to work to regulate the pull on local medical services. When young girls get pregnant multiple areas of their lives suffer, from education to employment and family issues. How do you impact a cultural construct that those involved may not want to change or recognize as a problem?

The cultural issues extend into City Hall.

"Mayor Spencer just had his State of the City speech. He mentioned monetizing the parking system. That's not the answer."

Reed believes the city spends money like it isn't in crisis.

"We had a conference of consultants, put them up in a hotel and catered the meals at a cost of $3,000. A second, larger group came in and the city spent $9,000 on it. Why not have these things at City Hall on the weekend? Order pizzas. Unplug the phones. This is taxpayer money we're spending."

In his speech, working language for the upcoming elections, Mayor Spencer also mentioned that the city will not "hand the keys" to Berks County.

"That's wrong." Reed says, "We're not enemies. It is wrong to villainize things and cut out the county. If we don't start handling the finances, Reading could easily go into receivership."

Receivership would place the Commonwealth of Pennsylvania in control of virtually all governmental decisions for the city. Elected officials would little say in most matters, including the fate of city assets, including all city-owned property and especially the water and parking authorities. City control would pretty much cease.

I ask Reed if this is a real possibility.

"I think it will happen. We aren't taking our money seriously. Everyone must give up some things and make their choices. Every wasted dollar is a liability. The State of the City speech itself cost $2,500 because we rented out the Goggle Works and catered it. Why not have it at City Hall? We operate in one of the most beautiful buildings in the area and should use it. That is wasted money. The city should lead by example."

Reed's mention of the Goggle Works reminds me of Adam Mukerji. He was thrilled to mention the new apartments built by the facility. I ask about them and their impact for the city.

"I hate to use this term, but we need some gentrification. We need some market rate housing. The minute Albert Boscov took HUD funding for that building, it opened it up to Section 8 residents. That drives away some of the people we need to move in and live to increase the tax base."

Boscov's heart is in it but, sometimes, Reed believes it may lead him astray in terms of the best end result. Reed personally had to vote against some of his renovation plans in the city. As a good friend, it was painful decision.

"You know, he could put a Boscov's back downtown. Not even a big store, just a Boscov's Express. Imagine what it could do, seeing that name back in Reading. We need long-term investment like that. We need to have the difficult conversations. You know that Fire and Ice Festival?" Reed asks.

The Fire and Ice Festival happened in January, a showcase of ice sculptures and events set up on Penn Street, funded by the Berks Community Foundation. She believes there needs to be more to investment than events.

"That money came from a grant, more than $50,000 dollars. At the Eagle, I worked for the family that funded the grant, the Quiers. I'll tell you this; I believe the patriarch would be spinning in his grave if he knew that money went to ice sculptures. And there will never be another Christmas tree like this past one."

The 2014 tree, an international headline, was a scraggly version of the traditional trees. It was tall, thin on greenery, and an embarrassment.

"Every story led with 'In the poorest city in the country…,' 'In the poorest city in the country...' I had one of my constituents call me the day it went up. She asked me how I could do this to her. The families, even if they are poor, are proud. The tree was an insult to their city, to their culture, she said. I promise you it will never happen again."

For the first time, I heard the bottom line of what failure could look like for Reading if things did not turn around. Berks County could step in and take over. Those fighting to make a difference on the governmental level would lose all influence. The power would be taken from the hands of those struggling to wield it well.

If that happened, as Reed theorized it would, she would be included. The City Council would be no more than a placeholder.

Until that day, she would continue fighting the battle, working the balance between advancement and responsibility.

Chapter 18

Deputy Warden of Treatment Stephanie Smith, Berks County Prison

I switch on my cell phone's navigation just in time to discover I had missed the road. Route 183 runs north and west of the city of Reading and my only experience on it is a handful of trips to Hawk Mountain in Kempton and Christmas Village in Bernville. Turn the opposite direction on the road and you'll find the newest building for St. Joseph's hospital, the location in which my wife spent almost forty hours of labor bringing Carter into the world.

The navigation had me turn left on Palisades Road and, immediately, I was in the woods surrounding Blue Marsh Lake. Blue Marsh is a reservoir built by the Army Corps of Engineers in 1979. It's a popular summer spot for picnics, hikes and bike rides.

In the midst of the rolling hills and idyllic atmosphere, you'll find Berks County Prison.

Snowflakes whip across my windshield as I turn up a maintenance road towards the parking area. I wait for a white pickup truck to move as it completes its task of plowing snow the shade of cigarette ash. It takes three passes of the lot to find an available parking space.

The lobby of the prison is a small room, a triangle of chairs facing a booth staffed by a guard. I walk up to his booth, surrounded in security glass, and start to speak.

"Shift change now buddy, I'll help you in fifteen or twenty minutes. Have a seat."

With no room to debate, I sit and watch a steady stream of correctional officers, counselors, and medical staff members arrive and depart from the bowels of the prison. I send my contact an email and, in tem minutes, she appears.

Stephanie Smith, Deputy Warden of Treatment, walks through the employee entrance. The lobby had filled with family members waiting to visit. She ushers me back to the administration area and I follow.

Berks County Prison is an odd mix of a century worth of construction. There are buildings from the early 1900's and parts constructed more than ninety years later. Smith's office is cut from the basement of a parent's house, dark wood paneling on the walls with file cabinets and a single cup coffee machine waiting for use. A black mug rests under the nozzle of the machine, red stirrer leaning against the edge. Smith offers me coffee as she composes her own cup.

After earning her Bachelor's degree in Psychology with a Criminal Justice focus at Alvernia University, Smith found herself with Berks Counseling Center. There she had her first exposure working with inmates returning to society. She completed her Master's degree spending time at Graterford Prison as a student. The advanced education led to a supervisory position at TASC, Treatment Access and Services Center of Berks County. Work outside the bars soon paled for the chances inside.

Now, Smith teaches two classes at Alvernia specializing in addictive behaviors, while holding a small private practice. Her main focus is the prison and the chance to make a difference in an underserved population. She started at Berks County Prison in September of 2014 and, in that relatively short period of time, has taken on a large amount of responsibility.

Smith has a warm personality, blonde hair cascading over a professional demeanor offset by a golden badge hanging from a chain around her neck. Her analytical mind quickly shows itself and the potential of her impact for the men and women of her prison.

"What happens if someone is up for release and they have nowhere to go?" I ask.

Smith sips her coffee.

"Our Probation and Parole Department manages the release of inmates. When they do get out, they must have a home plan. We need to know where they'll be."

The prison houses a variety of inmates, all working through sentences around two years in duration.

"Unpaid child support carries a ninety day sentence," Smith tells me, "some inmates are unsentenced and waiting for trial and they have no idea how long they'll be here. We even have people here for traffic tickets."

Smith and her staff try their best to equip inmates for release. They identify treatment needs, provide applications for medical assistance, and bring as many community services inside the prison as possible. Some inmates will be released to Hope Rescue Mission, even though the prison tries to avoid it.

A key part of the facility is the Reentry Center located down the hill from the prison. Families are invited to come in and work with the outgoing inmates who have finished their sentences. Here, the counselors put on finishing touches to the process started while the inmate is still inside.

When a new prisoner enters the prison, they will meet Smith's staff for the first time. "We do a need assessment at intake," Smith says, "and we try to help with essential things like cognitive skills. We offer groups and can make drug and alcohol referrals. The prisoners can refuse the treatment, but they will lose some incentives that go with it."

When prisoners reach the level of the Reentry Program, they must get the therapeutic help or be sent back to the main jail.

"We have stress and anger assistance for anyone convicted of a violent crime. Eighty percent of the population here is related to drug issues."

The prison houses approximately 1,200 inmates. That means almost a thousand prisoners need help to escape their addictions.

"Poverty equals stress. Stress heads to addictive behaviors to manage the stress. Addiction is a disease but not something like cancer. You can be arrested for your addictions. Jail can destroy a family. You have jobs and income loss. We used to incarcerate people out of fear, now we do it in anger."

Smith believes in the power of diversion and that it is a good thing for Berks County. This is the base level of combating crime and poverty in Reading. Smith's oversight extends to counselors, caseworkers, the medical department, chaplain, education and GED prep programs, and the Reentry Center.

I ask about Graterford Prison. The name loomed up from my childhood. I had grown up in the town just next to Graterford. It is a maximum security facility, housing some of the most dangerous inmates in the state. Smith used her experience inside those walls to impact the programs at Berks County.

"Graterford houses almost 3,500 people comparted to our 1,200. They operate on a grand scale. Their prisoners have more movement. Ours are locked down the majority of the day. My car was searched more than once driving in and out, and I was a student there. The prisoners would work outside in the summer and you'd see guards riding horses and carrying shotguns."

If inmates at Berks County Prison pass the two year mark, they must go to a state facility. Smith is constantly examining her population. If an inmate could do better somewhere else, a transfer request is put in. The state prisons offer more options. The county prison is Smith's world and, even though the time is less, she makes the most of it. She has the answers needed to defend the daily operations of the prison, a valuable asset when tax payer money is funding the process.

"We need to bridge the gap for outgoing inmates. They should have medical assistance turned on the day they are released. We should be able to apply for assistance and have it in a suspended state until the inmate is released. Insurance is the major key for medical, addiction, and mental health service needs."

Smith's focus is on the impact of rehabilitation. She sees opportunity past the punishment.

"We do not have enough people out there for the facilities available. Long term support is needed. We have things like Easy Does It, the YMCA, Camp Joy, and SAM. Even with these programs, there are inadequate resources. When someone gets released, there's a thirty to sixty day wait for outpatient treatment. TASC tries to assist when they can."

There is a stigma about prison. Smith wants the public to know it is a place of opportunity. Cynicism is hard to break. The prison system, like the nonprofits and charities, must have real goals. Smith wants a day where the prison would not need to exist because of real and vital change.

"We have a great staff of counselors here to help. Not everyone is 'bad or scary.'" There are families seeing the prison as the enemy who has taken their loved ones.

"It is easy for families to be mad at the jail. We only do what the judge tells us to do when they order someone held. We need to educate people and reach out to the community. If something is happening at the home, we want to know about it. I give people my direct number all the time. They can call me and I'll get the message to the inmate. We want to see people do well here. I always think about what I can do to prep people for release."

Smith has categories for the people that enter the prison.

"First we have a low group. Not a lot of help is needed or done because it may even be harmful. We have the top group. These people are violent and unwell; nothing can be done to help them. Last we have the middle group. They can be helped and will change. We always tell people that we need to bridge the gap between here and their first day home."

In an office surrounded by those deemed unable to be in society, I imagine the skeletons that could hang in Smith's closet.

"We make sure we have boundaries set up. I mean, these are your neighbors out there. You will run into them at the grocery store. I have coworkers who run into people all the time."

The prison is actively building connections with local high schools and colleges, offering observation and learning opportunities.

"You know, I never wore a badge before here," Smith says as she picks up the one hanging on the chain around her neck, "they see this and think automatically that I'm a cop. Some try to pull things over on me. I'd like to think it's hard, but they'll keep trying. If I can just get them thinking about change, to not give up and make the effort. That's what we can do."

The old ways of detention have failed, Smith believes. Being tough on crime only made jail an accepted responsibility in communities slammed with poverty. They believe it comes with the territory.

"We need to incarcerate less and help more people as people," Smith says. "What can I do to stop you from getting out and going to that bad place? What is the key? Is it medical? Mental health? Say someone has bad teeth and no insurance. The pain gets bad enough that they rob someone to get money to buy the painkillers on the street. Now, they're back when we could have gotten the medical help to stop the cycle in the first place."

The connection after release is where poverty causes the biggest problem. Smith tries to reinforce needs with staff working on job placement for inmates. Entry-level jobs won't provide enough income for living wages. Inmates may need two entry-level jobs, or at least one with a higher wage.

"We need to provide hope and diversion. We don't want to keep seeing the same people here again and again."

Smith's holistic approach can be derailed quickly by mental health issues. If the prison sets a level of care, only to see it drop at release with insurance issues, they've lost progress.

"Our staff here is highly trained to deal with mental health issues. Our officers have forty hours of training a year for crisis intervention, de-escalation, and suicide prevention. We tell them their best tool is their mouth. You know how you see, on television, those extraction teams of six guys dressed in tactical gear? They charge into cells and remove prisoners. Our teams consist of two guards, highly trained, each with body cameras. Their extractions rarely lead to violence."

This forward thinking has made Berks County Prison a certified training academy, one of the only facilities with that designation in the area.

"I tell every inmate I see that they are not here for a life sentence. They are getting out. They must keep that in mind as we prepare them to go back into the community."

Smith is consistently professional, courteous, and caring. Incarceration operates in a cyclical nature, one which those working at the prison attempt to break. They provide value and hope to people who may have lost it.

The shift in focus from punishment to diversion is one that has the potential to make a real difference. The prison in Berks County operates outside the world of the charities and nonprofits. They are their own island, situated in the woods twenty minutes away from the city. If Smith's ideas continue to grow and come to fruition, it will become a bastion of hope for the community. One day it will be seen as a chance to make things better, not just a part of urban life.

Chapter 19

CEO Peter Barbey, Reading Eagle Company

As I cross the Penn Street Bridge, rain cuts through the slate sky. The city was struggling to pull itself out of winter with this morning a strong invitation to sleep in. I navigate to the parking garage on the corner of 3rd and Court Street, due to meet with Peter Barbey, CEO at the *Reading Eagle Company* in roughly fifteen minutes.

The *Reading Eagle* building takes up a block of space that contains a commercial printing company, media, advertising, and internet services. Through the tinted windows of the lower floors, you can see sheets of paper run through the presses, a shade of journalism from years before. I enter to find a security guard seated at a desk uncomfortably close to the door itself.

A pair of elevators waits behind her and I punch the button to head up to the second floor. The interior of the space is a study in Art Deco design with metallic accents and dark lines, calling back again to a time when journalists did their work without the luxury of digital distribution.

The elevator doors open to reveal a lobby of painted wood, antique chairs, a wooden table and two copies of the newspaper. Beverly, Barbey's assistant, meets me at the corner. She disappears and returns a minute later to tell me that he is ready. As I follow her to the executive area, it was like stepping into a scene from *Mad Men*.

The center of the room has a set of large desks with similar wood fronts and metal accents. Barbey stands in front of a Keurig making a cup of coffee.

"Can I get you any?" he asks.

I ask for tea.

"Want anything in it?"

I tell him I take it straight.

"Me too. Follow me." I follow him to the corner of the room and into his office.

Rain taps against the windows overlooking Penn Street. A framed black and white picture of Frank Sinatra in a recording studio hangs to the right of the window. Two more frames held issues of *Business Weekly* and *Berks Country*, both offshoots of the paper created in the last four years of Barbey's tenure.

We sit at a small table in front of Barbey's desk. His family is native to Berks County for more than two centuries. They founded the Vanity Fair Outlets (the first outlet stores in the United States) and the Sunshine Beer Company. His interest in Reading, from a son of the area background, provides a unique lens into the current situation.

"Reading is exceptional in the case of an isolated city in a geographic sense. The roads we need aren't connected. Reading needs a line to I78," Barbey tells me. He is a student of history with knowledge reaching back to the environment of his forefathers.

"Reading is a vibrant 20th Century City. The problem is that model is harder to sustain in a postindustrial time. We have a good base for small industry. Industry rolls through. It always happens here."

The companies once inside the city lines have found ways to the suburbs.

"We are still a unified community."

Barbey asks me where I am from and I tell him Montgomery County, about thirty miles southeast of the Reading. "We have a 'Bersky' culture. You haven't been up here a long time and I'm sure you've seen it. Reading was once the capital city for Germans in the eastern United States. The Pennsylvania Dutch was headquartered here before they shifted to Lancaster."

The newspaper published a German language edition until 1909 with the advent of World War I. No one, at that point, wanted to be walking the streets reading a German paper.

"We need the immigrant cycles here. The Italians, Europeans, Polish, they all moved through to run the local businesses." The population around the city is not concerned with European immigrants at the moment.

The focus has shifted to the massive influx of Latino immigration.

"Latino and Black assimilation is two totally different things at this moment. Reading will heal the racial problem when we can see past image." Barbey had lived out in Arizona for years. "A friend of mine in Arizona married a beautiful and intelligent Latino woman. You go to a party in Arizona and the crowd thinks, 'Wow, look at her.' You put her in a party in Wyomissing and people will say, 'What's that Latino woman doing here?'"

The issues of race and poverty are often intertwined in the mindset of the population. The bottom-line problem is this; how does one to change the viewpoint of an entire city? How do you shift mindsets of the surrounding communities who feel that Reading is not their problem?

"You know, when those poverty numbers came out in 2011, my gut reaction was that it was weird. Reading didn't read that way.

Last summer, we decided to look into it. The metric for poverty is based on the National Average Poverty Rate, the Poverty Threshold and Cost of Living Calculation. So what does that do?" Barbey asks me in the spirit of the leader of a journalism empire.

Tying cost of living into the equation was the final card to fall.

"If things like gas, goods, and childcare are cheap, then you end up on the poverty list. Reading is one of the most affordable places to live in America. We actually called the people at MIT who worked on the formulas to talk about it. They acknowledged the issue but it will not be corrected. There's too much money involved from the cities on the other end of the spectrum."

When the headline was released, it hit and stayed even through the efforts of people like Barbey who are in position to broadcast the underlying truth.

"Reading is a good place to come if you are poor. We have a lot of single mothers because of the availability of assistance here. It is one of the few cities in the area you can sell your food stamps to someone who needs them more on the street."

The problems with the city may even stem the formation of Pennsylvania itself.

"Pennsylvania is a Commonwealth. One thing that means is that we cannot annex municipalities. When I lived out in Phoenix, if you looked at the history of the place, it started small. If they needed help, they just annexed a surrounding neighborhood into the city limits. Suddenly, you had an increased tax base and funds. We can't do that here, even though the surrounding neighborhoods are part of Reading, whether they want to say it or not. You've heard of the 'donut.'?"

I've grown accustomed to the illustration by now, the image of Reading as the hole in the midst of the surrounding towns.

"We can't annex the donut."

Barbey is quick to illustrate all aspects of the problem. Reading has found its way into the current situation not entirely of its own volition. This knowledge angers him as a member of the media. He cannot stand when blame is pointed wrong direction.

"There will always be poor and addicted people. We've taken a glass jar," Barbey opens his hand, holding the imaginary jar. He slowly turns it over. "And trapped the poor where they are, and then we act like it is the only problem."

Put Act 47 restrictions on top of the jar and you multiply the problems.

"See, here's the thing. You can only keep triaging the issues for so long. We have a handful of people trying to triage the issues until retirement. They think, let's see…" he turns to his wristwatch, "I only have a few more years to go. The problem then gets passed to the next generation. If I was under fifty years old, I'd be pissed."

I mention the figurative "Toyota plant" economic savior that has been mentioned in more than one conversation. The causes behind it not happening ranged from education to space, taxes, and financial base.

"Toyota has happened," Barbey said, "it has. It happened when Penn State Hershey purchased St. Joseph's Hospital." Penn State had recently acquired one of the two major health players in the city. The new hospital building sits just up the highway with a mass of open land around it.

"Reading Hospital should be nervous. There was a point where they made a ton of money. Now things are shifting. Penn State is the largest health provider in the state and they have room to expand. Medical is the Toyota factory." Even with lower wages, doctors and other staff could live in Berks County in a comfortable status.

The question of employment connects clearly with education.

"Reading School District has a huge problem. Now, we have the Hill School in Pottstown and I always wondered why we don't have a private school here. We do, it is Wyomissing. Wyomissing is like a private school. The school district relies on private assistance from the tax base and it just isn't there. Reading needs help but we can't blame the kids."

Local gangs recruit from the schools. They need kids who, if caught, will only face juvenile records that can vanish when they turn eighteen. There will always be a link between crime and poverty, Barbey believes, and a cultural attraction in the current environment.

"We need more proper policing. Act 47 factored out the police force. Look at York (a city near central Pennsylvania). They have more police than we do. Right now we have officers in cruisers and not on the street. They are running to crimes, not preventing them. We were doing well back when the arena opened (now the Santander Bank Arena). Restaurants popped up and we had officers on horseback. Now money gets cut, businesses leave, the police are gone and millions of dollars are lost. You cut the police to save money and end up losing more money in the hit against the tax base with the vacating businesses."

The push back has come too hard and now Reading is scrambling to recover. I ask Barbey about the future and the paper's responsibility to the city. A conversation is needed and voices are straining to be heard.

"Newspapers will always exist as long as the market need exists, as long as there is a need for community." Certain surrounding metro areas are struggling for readers. Barbey shows me a document hanging on his wall with readership rates. Reading's numbers show the lowest decline. Some outside areas are even giving out copies for free in an effort to obtain every last shred of business.

"People need a reason for unity, something to unite for. The tide will be turning for Reading and now we need to make the right choices. I was shocked at the challenge we faced in engaging residents outside the city, in changing the perception of crime here. It happens just as much out there as it does here."

The lack of engagement will serve as an anchor keeping Reading well below its potential. We must, at some point, realize it is everyone's problem.

"Do you know we have no developers coming into the city? There are two in Reading, Alan Shuman and Albert Boscov. Shuman is private. Boscov mixes private funds with public money.

That's it. The situation with the roads hurts us here too. I often wonder if the founders thought that it was an advantage to be cut off from New York. We could make our own money here, run our own businesses, and keep it to ourselves," Barbey says.

He is ready to move the newspaper deep into the future. They are working to expand into the surrounding areas outside of Berks County. His passion is to tell the stories in and around Reading and to share available resources. At the moment, *Reading Eagle Company* owns the vertical stack of distribution. They can do print, web, and marketing work. Facebook likes will disappear, Barbey tells me, and eventually those readers will fade away. He believes a multi-tiered approach, similar to the ones available through his company, are the answer.

"When I went to publish *Business Weekly* people told me it was a dumb idea, that there would be nothing to write about. It is still going strong. I did *Berks Country* and it makes us more money than the website. That's a print magazine making more than digital. Print isn't dead. It's not going anywhere."

Barbey's personality is engaging. We had spanned almost two hours of conversation and we could have kept going. He has ideas and views flowing deeper through the problems. He's telling the story of digging out a new mindset and civil respect.

"So, your premise isn't necessarily wrong. It's just not totally correct. Reading isn't the poorest city in the country as the metric for that study was flawed. We do have major issues though and it is a poor city. I said to Governor Corbett that Reading is the perfect experiment. You can drop $5 million here and see immediate results. Try that in Philadelphia or Pittsburgh and it will make no difference."

We shake hands again and Barbey offers to send me some recent articles that the paper had written about poverty. I take a final sip of my tea that had gone cold.

"The story you want to tell is that Reading is every city. We are a glass jar city. Our story is the one of every city."

As the man heading the mouthpiece of the city, Barbey is helping to guide it to a new and better future. There will always be a need for community and new conversation where real and valuable change is found.

Until then, the glass jar remains and the pressure continues.

Chapter 20

Berks County Sheriff, Eric Weaknecht

The front of the Berks County Courthouse is covered with scaffolding. Two separate blocks have walkways sectioned out under the scaffolds and, for a moment, I am safe from the afternoon rain. I pass the main entrance once and turn the corner, stopping at a side door with a sign telling me to go back the way I came.

Traffic weaves in and around the narrow section of Court Street.

The entrance to the building is dark, recessed lighting struggling against the gloom from outside. A pair of security guards monitor a metal detector. The sheriff's office is on the third floor of the building, a fraction of the way towards the top of one of the tallest structures in the city. I take the stairs, dodging employees who are finishing their days.

The door to the office creaks and two officers look up. I tell them I'm there for Sheriff Weaknecht. They ask me to have a seat on a wooden bench that shifts under my weight. The officer that told me to sit picks up the phone and starts a new conversation.

"Yes, you sent in a check for twelve dollars. The fine on the case was actually twenty-two…"

The office is a buzz of activity with papers getting filed and a shift change starting into the evening. After a few minutes Theresa, the Sheriff's assistant, ushers me down the hall.

There is no glamour here.

The walls are a drab pale color with wanted posters and public notices hanging at variable locations. The men and women of the office are the engine that processes every arrest made in Berks County. We turn left and, after another set of doors, Sheriff Eric Weaknecht waits with an outstretched hand.

His office is a study in cool blues and slightly disheveled at the moment as it gets a new carpet. He wears a blue Oxford shirt without a tie. As we start talking, he shifts in his seat.

Weaknecht's career in law enforcement began in 1984 at twenty years old, finding his way into the elected position of Berks County Sheriff in 2007. He saw no other option and is a prime example of passion chased and lived out.

"We handle two sides here at the Sheriff's office," he tells me, "crime and civil. When bills can't be paid, rent can't be paid, even with credit card debts we may have to step in." The idea of a warrant for credit debt is scary in the current economic condition. As Weaknecht speaks, his personality is disarmingly warm and open.

"Every arrest in Berks County is processed downstairs. We serve warrants and sell civil property." Many homebuyers look in Sheriff's Sale section of the newspaper more than once when considering their first home. "As the local police departments have dealt with budget issues and cuts, we are only getting busier."

Weaknecht goes to his desk and produces a folder of information. He had prepared numbers for our interview.

"Our volume is up across the board. In terms of total arrests," he flips pages in his report, "We had 8,000 in 2010 and 8,327 in 2013. Court appearances between 2011 and 2013 increased by almost a thousand. In 2011 we had 502 sheriff-sold homes. In 2013 we sold 750 homes. See, people don't anticipate the burden of property taxes here."

His point is valid, even if Berks County is on the cheaper side of things. When wages don't match and local influences drive up taxes, homeowners are squeezed.

"A property is either sold with a lien on it, like a mortgage, or sold free and clear. If it sits for a while, the bank may move to a free and clear sale. For those, we sold 717 in 2011. In 2013 we sold 1,200. We've even seen a major increase in civil action from credit card companies."

Weaknecht acknowledges a clear connection between crime and poverty.

"In 2011 we issued 3,700 warrants. In 2013 we had 4,800. The numbers for 2014 aren't complete yet, but we fully expect an even more drastic increase across the board." This increase comes with a decrease in manpower for the city. Officers are now running from call to call in response, not preventative policing.

"We have a great relationship with Reading. We work well together with their department and we want to share resources as much as possible, even outside the city." Weaknecht is concerned with relationships as they are the key to keeping officers and civilians safe. "If we know there is a section with hot calls for a time we will be sure to help out. We'll do role call and send people there. I want them to be present, to have cars on the street."

This is not an easy time for law enforcement, with the events of Ferguson, Missouri and the repeated instances of violence and protest against police. I ask about the challenge and if the image of police can ever be recovered.

"We need a top down change in viewpoint of law enforcement. I mean, from national government all the way down to local. People need to let the process take place. We should defend the process and not assign guilt prematurely. Let the process work and, after someone is found guilty, you protest all you want. I think law enforcement, including myself, should be held to a higher standard. We can't uphold and break the law at the same time," Weaknecht says.

I ask if he'd ever had an instance that shook him to where he'd taken it home.

"We had a Dominican Day parade here one year that required a significant show of force. Thankfully, nothing serious happened. The best thing to do is plan for the worst and pray for the best. The problem is that we have no more casual conversations. You have an officer on the street where, at one time, someone approaching to talk would be normal. Now it is viewed with suspicion. We need to change that."

Poverty often carries with it a host of issues from mental illness to addiction. When these combine, you have a tragic situation as with the murder of Deputy Kyle Pagerly in June 2011. While responding to a call, Pagerly was gunned down by a suspect dealing with a myriad of problems.

"I was so impressed with the community's response to that," Weaknecht says, "people took off work and lined the streets. When the service went from the arena over to Spring Township, people lined the streets and held American flags. It was amazing." Pagerly's wife was three months pregnant at the time. "His daughter is doing well. We spoil her as much as possible."

His eyes flicker with emotion.

I ask about the school district. There have been years in the city with multiple children taken through violence and crime.

"We need to establish a rapport with a child. They need to know they can come to us for help. We have an Explorer post in Reading School District. We just had this young girl who won our Sheriff's Award. She started off really shy and wouldn't say anything. At the end, you need to execute a felony traffic stop to graduate. You should have heard her yelling commands and taking charge of the situation. It was amazing."

Weaknecht has two children himself, a stepson who had found his way into law enforcement and a step daughter who, by his own admission, he would never advise to take the same path. It is not a job for everyone, especially in a city fighting to change its image.

"We've had our family in here many times for events. We've parked at the arena, walked to the Peanut Bar, had dinner, and went to the show. We've never had any problems. Now, you have to remember, criminals prey on the weak. You need to keep an eye on what you do and where you are. If you're walking around looking over your shoulder and looking unsure, you put yourself out there. I wouldn't go to Front Street at two in the morning," Weaknecht tells me.

Reading's position geographically is about an hour and a half away from New York City. Drive around and you'll often see a group of New York license plates. There is an evident connection.

"We do have drug traffic coming down from New York. These people have no intention to work or make the city better. Here's where we need to have the drug arrests and it becomes a challenge when manpower is cut. The criminals are resourceful, believe me."

Weaknecht's territory is all of Berks County. This includes land that ranges from city to country and small town. His staff will see a variety of situations and experiences.

"There are a few agencies in Berks County with less than ten guys. They need more aggressive assistance and face a huge burden. Just last weekend we sent six deputies up to Kutztown to help break up a party we had found out about beforehand. I think some of these police departments end up putting themselves out of business. You have the unions that go to arbitration and then they're stuck. There are fewer cops in Berks County now than there was in 2007."

It takes a second for that to sink in.

In a city that needs help to turn things around, to drive out the crime and bad influences, there is a need for more presence on the streets, not less.

"We've had major cuts across the board. Politics are way too deeply involved." The environment has shifted in Weaknecht's thirty-one years in law enforcement. He mentions a rising star in Berks County, District Attorney John Adams.

"Adams is doing a great job with this ARD Program." Accelerated Rehabilitation Disposition, he explains, offers an offender a chance to have a crime wiped from their record after a successful period of assistance and not reoffending. If they slip up, the prior crime is added to the case and the punishment stiffer. It has helped to keep the numbers down from the prison population.

"Prison is not for everyone. There are people who can be helped and turn their lives around. Some, though, they offend three, four, five times and maybe they need to spend time incarcerated. It is really specific to the person."

Weaknecht will be at the office late this evening handling other administrative matters. The department never closes, booking arrests through the night. They even have a judge on call if needed. Forty holding cells wait in the basement of the court house, often filled by the functioning Night Court.

In a time when culture seems stacked against law enforcement, Weaknecht serves as a qualified ambassador to the job. Berks County is fortunate to have his leadership in such a vital area.

Sirens sound in the distance, a constant noise this afternoon. Law enforcement is doing its work, hampered by the economy like everything else in this city. With Weaknecht in the lead, it will continue to find success and be a positive force for change in a vital time. In time it can, and will, serve to shift the mindset and turn the tide against crime and negativity in Reading.

Chapter 21

Berks County Commissioner, Christian Leinbach

As I stood in the office of Mercy Community Crisis Pregnancy Center, a family spoke with a volunteer about their troubles. She advised them to contact Commissioner Leinbach's office.

He was the one who *handled problems*.

On a brisk morning in March, one with a hint of the sleet and late-season snow that would arrive that afternoon, I set off to meet Commissioner Leinbach. His office is located in the County Services Center, a large structure of sixteen floors that houses county courts and a variety of human services agencies like Children and Youth, Aging, and Mental Health. The County Services building connects to the County Courthouse with walkways on the second, third, and fourth floors. I wander around the Public Defender offices before realizing I am on the wrong side.

The bank of elevators eventually opens and allows me to journey to the thirteenth floor. I step off the elevator into a modern lobby and waiting area. The board room for the commissioners stands in darkness to my right. A pair of windows provides a panoramic view of the city.

The officials on this floor are tasked with governmental policy making and enforcement for all of Berks County. Those struggling on the streets look so far away at this height. Cars drive to and from jobs. Construction workers operate on a roof below. I admire the view until it is time for our meeting.

Leinbach wears a white shirt with a soft purple tie, composed and put together. I had interviewed other government officials at this point and, by far, his image is the closest to my expectations. He ushers me inside.

"I entered into this job with the attitude that you can't be successful by saying 'no'. I needed to solve problems. You know how, with the Senate, there needs to be a majority? It used to be fifty-one, but now they need sixty. Here the magic number is two. There are three of us so all we need is two to agree and make something happen."

Leinbach, elected in January 2008, is tasked with executing state and federal programs in Berks County in a multitude of areas like Children and Youth Services, Aging Services, and other programs.

"We are here to serve the public. We can't pick and choose." He types into a small netbook computer on his desk. "I want to read you something from Proverbs, chapter 31." Leinbach is a church elder and a man of faith. His background and belief system carries him forward in his position.

He quotes two verses where King Lemuel is recounting what he learned from his mother.

"'Speak up for those who cannot speak for themselves, for the rights of all who are destitute. Speak up and judge fairly; defend the rights of the poor and needy.' I came across that passage a few years after taking office," he says, "I knew it was my job to give voice to those who are defenseless, to the poor and needy. I needed to look out for them. I wanted to make sure that people without political voice get justice and we have a level playing field."

In his time, Leinbach has seen the growth and development of some valuable outreach programs.

"Hope Rescue Mission has really turned around under Rob Turchi over the last four years. We are having the ribbon cutting for Camp Joy soon. That's a facility for drug and alcohol rehabilitation. There are places like Mercy Community Crisis Pregnancy Center and Easy Does It. These programs are great assets for Reading and Berks County."

It wasn't always moving like this.

"In the early 20th Century, the church was greater than the government in terms of involvement in social welfare. The church pushed for those values you read in James, the whole 'Faith without works is dead' line. Government eventually stepped in and created dependent generations with reversed ideas of social welfare."

Suddenly, the work part of the equation didn't matter, for better or worse. He believes most will say it is the government's responsibility.

"Our church sent a team down to Haiti after their major earthquake with bags of supplies. The local church leaders had lists of those families really in need. The crowds would gather and, if someone came up for supplies and they didn't need it, they were waved away. Could you imagine that kind of thing here?" Leinbach believes the church should know the community better than government.

"We've created a modern day plantation system with a society of dependents, not independents."

Following his passion for community involvement, Leinbach and his wife, along with several educators and parents began King's Academy, a school near Centerport in northern Berks County. It has no permanent church affiliation and currently houses more than two hundred students with the involvement of more than fifty churches.

He believes there are valuable examples, like the school, of unity between faith communities.

"In reality, our issues are not that different from other similar locations. I will say this; crime is overblown by the *Reading Eagle*. Before we had the Crime Summit, we had a meeting in this office with District Attorney John Adams. We told them their numbers were wrong and they went forward anyway."

Headlines, right or wrong, will sell copies.

"There's no wall around the city of Reading. It is spilling out into the suburbs. They are all part of the community. Politically, Reading is not a Republican city. It is a hotbed of Democratic votes. We need to realize the politics don't matter."

Leinbach is conscious of the territory. A focus on Reading, even with its pull on the area, can be detrimental. He believes the far ends of the county can be forgotten in the turmoil.

"You know what the problem is? They did a study and found that people outside Berks County don't know who we are. They don't know our identity. We've changed our name so many times that it hurts us. Now, it's the Greater Reading area. What does that mean? If you focus on 'Greater Reading' you'll miss places like Boyertown, Hamburg, and Hawk Mountain. We need to keep in mind the assets around us."

The Act 47 determination for the city has been an issue of repeated concerns. It weighs down public officials and programs struggling to survive.

"As far as I know, no city in Pennsylvania placed in Act 47 has ever recovered. Reading will go bankrupt without radical changes. We have horrible leadership in the city right now (Mayor Vaughn Spencer and his administration), the worst it has had in years and it is not solely their fault. They're using one time cash fixes for bigger problems. They just floated a bond issue and took out loans that drew them deeper into it. I mean, the city has a brutal history. You can't pull yourself out if things don't change."

Government bankruptcy programs are not the same as private ones, he tells me, and the city would not be totally off the hook for obligations. If Reading does declare bankruptcy and things don't change, they'll be right back where they started.

"Politics are a bigger issue in this city. Strings are tied to the money that comes in. Unions are doing serious damage. Now, most of our employees are union and they are great workers. It is not them, it's their leadership."

I ask, off the record, if any people or agencies are pushing their limits legally. I say that I'll cap my pen and I do so as I finish the question.

"You can uncap the pen," Leinbach tells me, "I'll tell you what I think. The current mayor (Vaughn Spencer) is completely in the pocket of the unions. It is damaging and costing the city a large amount of money. Just look at the recent sewer plant agreement. That was a reward for union money. Their budgets are paid for by employee and city contributions, and then they push back on the people paying them in the first place."

There are other answers being thrown around at the state level. Property tax is debated at the moment and often fodder for election season. Leinbach doesn't support the idea in any form as no one really owns their home or business if they are tied to a property tax and that the amount often does not reflect your ability to pay it.

"When you rely on property tax, you end up with odd situations." The first example coming to mind is the school district, funded with property tax money.

"In Reading, 37% of the properties are tax exempt. I'm talking government buildings, the federal court building, schools, churches, and even those luxury apartments down by the Goggle Works." The apartment building was funded by Albert Boscov, founder of the Boscov's department store chain and local resident. In the midst of the luxury building, he placed twelve Section 8 and HUD units after accepting government funds. The placement of these units allowed for the tax exemption.

"We fought them on it. We turned down their tax exempt request and they appealed. They won and we took it to Commonwealth Court where the verdict was upheld. Now all that money from property tax on that building is gone. I love Albert and what he does for the city, but it was the wrong choice. I'm just waiting to see when the tax exempt request will come from that new hotel on Penn Street."

It is an example of money and politics attempting to squeeze the blood from a city that is anemic. The change, if and when it happens, must be at the deepest levels.

"This crime-riddled perspective is false. Talk to District Attorney Adams and you'll hear how it isn't true. The visitor's bureau did a study that showed that people visiting Berks County and Reading felt Reading was safer than other similar cities in our region." Leinbach has walked the streets at multiple times since taking office in 2008. "I live in northern Berks County. Honestly, my concern level here at night is the same as if I'd walk in the woods by my house at night."

I ask for his best and worst-case projections over the next five years.

"This city needs non-partisan, independent leaders. We won't turn it all around, but it can happen. We need stability with visionary thinking. In terms of the worst case, the city goes bankrupt and must start all over. You have to remember, any crisis provides opportunity. Mistakes aren't mistakes if you learn from them. Change happens when you wake up and decide you've had enough."

In Leinbach's vision, everyone in the city is family, from residents to workers and business owners. Every member of the family deserves a seat at the table.

"I go back to Proverbs 31. We need to look out for those not like us and not just for politics. My job is to be a servant, to fight for justice."

Would the city recover? Did this whole process have a happy ending? Or was the happy ending a bankruptcy and a new start?

These problems exist in all cities and are regulated on some level. In Reading's case, they pushed the city to a depth of poverty. It will only surface with deep and profound changes.

Chapter 22

General Manager Craig Poole, Hilton DoubleTree Hotel

I jog across the parking lot, get in my car, and speed down route 10. The sun casts a blanket of warmth that is a blessing against the long winter. I am running late to a lunch meeting at *Jimmy Kramer's Peanut Bar* with Craig Poole, the General Manager of the new DoubleTree Hotel in construction on Penn Street.

When I arrive, a waitress leads me to his table as the "Gimme Shelter" from the Rolling Stones plays over the sound system.

Poole wears a dark blazer with the cuffs from his suit shirt sneaking under his sleeves. He is a warm personality filled with caring and hospitality. His voice is deep, barely hiding a trace of the western Pennsylvania of his childhood.

A waitress appears and he orders the special.

"I'm from Pittsburgh," Poole says, "I've changed a few neighborhoods out there. I've worked with multiple displaced hotels and repositioned them into a successful market. By success, I mean the properties next to them go from selling for $11,000 to $250,000. I read about Reading, came out and visited, and knew I wanted to be here."

His first stop was the Crowne Plaza in Wyomissing. He spent four years there and changed the face of the organization. The Crowne Plaza actively holds events for the community and Poole is a vital part of this engagement.

"When I got here, I started walking the streets. I wanted to figure things out, see why things are the way they are. I wanted to get the temp from store owners." Poole's territory is the Penn Street corridor. His hotel will draw a large amount of people and he wants to create the best possible surroundings for his future guests. Money coming in must stay in the community and, if not spent in the city, it will make way to the suburbs

"We've created a society dependent on social systems. In many ways, it is over benevolent. I wanted to talk with people and find out why they want to be enabled. I've found out that people care and the movement is shifting from negative to positive. People here are engaged in the homeless issue."

As a businessman, Poole consistently examines the bottom line. What is happening to all the supplies that are donated to the charities in the city? Are we creating the right world? He calls it an Under Bridge economy.

"Too many are dependent on a handout," he says.

Poole's business is done the old-fashioned way.

"I show up and meet people one on one. I do this because it needs to be done. We all want to make it." The small shop on the corner is important to the success of the hotel, just as much as the large chain store. He is vested in each business.

A recent news article had criticized the amount of tax free property in the city. The more places that don't pay, the more the economy suffers.

"Tax free can be good and bad. It can be seed money. Take a place like the Goggleworks. They could expand with the money their saving. Tax free can also be dangerous."

Poole is also a man of self-assessment.

"We always have to ask ourselves what is your contribution? Do we want to put our money here, in these places? The city needs non tax exempt businesses. The GoggleWorks was needed too, even with being tax free."

One of the places Poole supports is Hope Rescue Mission. He believes in the purpose and people behind it and is a part of talks to obtain a community building that is open post shelter hours. The men need to be out of the building at 8 a.m. He wants them to have a place to go. Idle hands can lead to the wrong road, especially in the world of poverty.

"No one has tried to tie a street together here. That's what I'm doing. I sit where the people sit. We need to listen to the people and see the value on the street." The normal process is to throw a program at a problem. Poole's world is simpler and direct.

"You ever hear the term fringe marketing? That's where I'm operating, out on the fringes. I want to work for the marginalized people. Take a company like Apple or CostCo. They are social capitalists. I'm a social capitalist. We need to be giving back to the community and use our talents to make a better world. "

While the clear solution to poverty seems to be money itself, that is not the case. Unity, on the community level, is the glue that keeps things together.

"When you see 501 c3's out there, and I mean ones committed to be non-profits, the people involved are good, but the organizations are selfish. There's no collaboration. Everyone wants their share of the money. You'll have two or three agencies working on one family. That's crazy. We need to join forces. If you don't join forces, you have no force."

I ask about the future of the city.

"It needs a radical shift. Now, radical shifts are sometimes the easiest thing to do. Take a place like *Mi Casa, Su Casa*," a restaurant in the city, "for them, a radical change is something as simple as staying open later into the night. It is good businesses buying bad businesses. It is a place like *Judy's on Cherry* building a coffee shop on Penn Street."

Judy's is a restaurant located a block behind Penn Street.

"Those businesses that survive here do so because they are making changes that are radical at the time. Something like taking a parking lot on 7th and Penn and turning it into a hotel." He mentions the hotel he will manage when construction is completed. The building, he estimates, will bring more than a half million visitors to the city in a year, with an income of more than $1 million for the city.

Poole cares for his hotel and the gateway neighborhood that surrounds it. He cares for the guests he has not met yet and their satisfaction when they book a room for a business trip or weekend.

"I tell business owners on this street. If they are not ready for this income, then it will leave and pass them by. Do they want the shops in Wyomissing getting rich or do they want it? I want people to win. The jobs that hotel brings will change this neighborhood."

Poole is motivation personified. If I were a local business, I'd take his suggestions and make changes. I'd want in on his vision of the future.

"Radical is achievable when we shift how we talk, behave, think, and believe. If you think something won't happen, then it won't. What you say will happen, will happen. You tell a kid they are bad and they'll believe it."

Businesses in the city are Poole's people, his version of the kids in his statement.

"Places like the *Peanut Bar* and *Judy's* are surviving. The people that just came on cut in at a bad time. They're looking at two choices, either move on or learn how to survive. We need to teach the entrepreneurs to make it. They must find their passions and then sell it."

As we wrap up, he tells me he is meeting with Sharon Parker from the Coalition to End Homelessness just after our conversation.

"I'm setting up an office at 5th and Penn. You know what I want to do? I want a desk outside. I'll set up a lawn chair and card table and put my laptop on there. I don't think there's a law against it. I'd love to get arrested for it, though. You know what's radical? Ghandi starting his walk across India, Martin Luther King facing down baseball bats and police dogs. Maybe one day you'll see me in the papers. When you read the story about a guy getting arrested for having his office on the street, you'll know who it is."

The street is in his blood and he has made it his own.

Poole's efforts are more than the hotel. They are changing the world outside. They are meeting people face to face and filling the empty seats. He offers advice to small businesses that would normally come at the hands of expensive advisors and college courses and he does it because he cares. He knows, in the end, his success is their success.

The rise of Reading will only happen if they join hands together and start taking steps to make it reality. Poole believes change is real and shows it every day that he hangs out in the area and speaks with the people. He hears what they have to say, argues if necessary, and educates in the end.

"Go out to the street and look around. You'll find me out there. It won't be too hard."

Chapter 23

President Alan Shuman, Shuman Development Group

The wind rips rain across the Lancaster Avenue Bridge as I maneuver through traffic. Trashcans and other debris skip over city streets. This added to the usual challenge of narrow roads and double parked drivers attempting to get as close as possible to their destinations. I cross Penn Street and turn on Washington, flanking the side of the M and T Bank building. It is a structure that stands out as curiously modern in a crowd of historical properties.

I park in the shadow of the Abraham Lincoln Hotel. The building was recently purchased by the man I will interview. It is a bastion of 1930's architecture, a taste of an era with different imagery, ideals, and economic conditions. I fight through the increasing rain as I skirt the outside of the building and enter a lobby of a concessions store, bank of elevators, and the bank itself.

The elevator quickly takes me to the fifth floor.

The carpets here are a mix of smooth yellow and red patterns, the furnishings of warm wood and glass. The logo of the Shuman Development Group spreads behind a desk at the far corner of the space and, at the moment, I can't find anyone. Just as I turn to wait by entrance, a man appears from a doorway to my right.

This is Alan Shuman, one of the only two developers inside the city of Reading, and today he is alone in his office. He ushers me into his boardroom and, for the second time in minutes, I pause. The walls of the room are glass, casting a view of the skyline and the slate clouds dropping rain on those walking below.

"This is an amazing space," I say.

"It had black trash bags over the windows when I bought it. We renovated the whole thing," he tells me.

We sit at a table that could easily hold thirty or forty people. Documents are spread across the length of the top. It feels like Shuman's personal office and the space is fitting for a man with such influence.

His main efforts in the city consist of purchasing historic and distressed buildings and renovating them to create opportunities.

"We pick out areas with a critical mass of properties. The spaces must have enough room to bring in jobs and create investment from the private sector. Many groups out there don't understand this part of urban development," Shuman says.

One of Shuman's recent projects was the Reading Outlet Center, more than 640,000 square feet of space. At the moment, he has a team cleaning out a building that was formally part of the Outlet Center. It will house a combination of apartments and commercial businesses.

He is an investor looking to gain maximum value on his purchases.

"One-off projects will not hit critical mass," he tells me. The city development has suffered under the strategy of one-off projects. "We need to understand the limited value of a single building. The city itself is not the challenge."

Part of the city is an issue, though.

"City Hall is a huge challenge. This is a Democratic city. There isn't one Republican in this administration. They are pro labor and union. I mean, the mayor is being sued by a non-union shop for the contract at the sewer plant. It was in the paper today."

Shuman has the resources to make a difference and he's facing an uphill battle.

"I have no lack of businesses. They are lined up to get in here. Take the Callowhill Building, for example," it is a topic he is passionate about, "I put in a proposal for that building. I had national businesses ready to go in. I'd keep it on the tax roll. I even offered to throw in $100,000 to help renovate the Pagoda. They gave it to Albert."

Albert Boscov stands on the opposite side of the aisle from Shuman. He has resources and pockets deepened by the chain of Boscov's Department Stores. He also takes government funds and tax credits, moving to make properties tax free. In a city with almost 40% tax free buildings, this can be deadly to the economy. Money from this lack of taxes will never hit the coffers that are already thin. The strategy uses tax payer money, something Shuman refuses to do.

I mention the apartment building at the GoggleWorks, a property that has come up in numerous conversations. It is the pride of the city, boasted by Adam Mukerji at the Redevelopment Authority and Mayor Spencer himself. Boscov, against the advice of the City Council, took government money and added a dozen apartments of Section 8 housing. This also allowed the building to gain tax free status.

"The Goggle Works building is a disaster. You have sixty units, worth say $60,000 per unit; you're talking about a building worth $3.6 million that the taxpayers paid $18.5 million to construct and it is off the tax rolls. The city owns the land under the building through an agreement with the Redevelopment Authority. The contracts are pro union, prevailing wage, and that money flows directly into city hall as campaign donations."

As he speaks, his voice picks up in volume.

"How about Entertainment Square? I bet they talked to you about that."

Entertainment Square is a set of businesses just across the Penn Street Bridge consisting of an IMAX movie theatre, restaurants, and other shops. It was another success according to the Redevelopment Authority.

"You ever go there?"

I tell him I haven't

"You ever drive through it? Try it one time. It's a fiasco. They have a sign up saying, 'We'll pay everything for new tenants.' That's unheard of and they still can't get people to get in there."

Shuman will never make the same offer. He requires a $10,000 deposit that is non-refundable. His tenants are invested from the beginning.

"I was talking to Rita's Ice this week. I have a pizza place ready to come in right now. People know you need to see me to get assets in the city. I am the way in. The city puts up too many roadblocks for new businesses and I am the only one who will help a small business work through them."

His cell phone rings. He pulls it from his pocket, checks the number, and motions that he has to take it. I only get one side of the conversation, a few mentions of a daycare and expansion. He ends the call after a minute and gestures to his pocket where he returned the phone.

"That's a great example of the problems in Reading. That's a daycare, one of my tenants. She's trying to expand. The city inspectors told her she needs one more bathroom to do it. We can't get city approval until May 7th to build one toilet. Other cities around here take seventy-two hours. Reading takes months. This is half-dozen jobs that could be created. I'm not getting rent on the property either, so I'm paying carrying costs. Reading is poor because of City Hall."

Shuman cares for his tenants.

"I could bring in 250 jobs a year myself if I had city support."

So why doesn't it happen? The logic end of the question waits in the air as the storm clouds roll by the window.

"I've faced years of waiting for zoning approval on projects. The carrying costs add up. A project in the city could easily be $500,000 in carrying costs alone."

The current push on Penn Street is the construction of the new DoubleTree hotel. I had spoken with Craig Poole, General Manager of the hotel, one week before this interview. I was curious, after getting such an honest response, of Shuman's opinion on the project.

"I think it will struggle. It is in a bad location. You know what's behind that building? Train tracks. I used to own the office building next to it. I've slept in that office building at night. The trains come through multiple times. What will happen when people experience that at the hotel? I heard that Albert had said he will call Norfolk Southern and tell them to not run their trains at night. I'll tell you this, I have a relative that works for Norfolk Southern and I asked him his opinion of Albert Boscov. He said they wouldn't even answer his phone call. Warren Buffet, maybe. Boscov? A guy who owns a few department stores? Not a chance."

On certain nights we can hear the trains running through from our bedroom window. If we can hear it from miles away, the hotel rooms will be loud.

"I bet they'll put in to make it tax exempt," Shuman says. It is an idea put forth by other sources like Commissioner Christian Leinbach. If they succeed, it will be another hurdle to fiscal stability.

Shuman's family emigrated from Germany to the area around the Oley Valley in Berks County in 1695, then migrated to Selingsgrove and Lewisburg before he returned in 1994. He wants to see this city turn around. The long-view result is a driving force.

"Reading is on the wrong path and it gets worse every year. We've seen a steady downturn over the past twenty years. Tax revenues don't make up for lowered property values. Not one property in this city has appreciated in value. I can't think of a single one. At some point you need to stop digging yourself a hole."

Shuman's believes the largest holes are from tax exemptions.

"That Callowhill Building is off the tax rolls. In 2010-2011 we saw the union jobs move out of City Hall and into the authorities. That bumped up all the utility bills. Some people are paying more for their water than their taxes. The authorities are all controlled by the unions with no oversight. It plays out on this image of big versus small and we need to meet in the middle."

There is an image of the city of Reading that pervades the surrounding communities, one of danger and insecurity. The key to changing things is shifting this spirit that has taken root in an area traditionally adverse to change.

"People don't like to take actions and make efforts. I'll give you two examples to consider. The first is a law firm that was right here," he points out the window to a building across the street. "They told me that their clients didn't want to come downtown, that, if they moved to Wyomissing, they would get more business. They moved and you know what happened? No increase at all."

"The second example is the Berks County Republican Party. They used to be based in the city. Their constituents told them, if they moved to the suburbs, they'd help them out more. They'd get more volunteers and assistance. They tried it for six years and the people didn't show up. I just moved them back into the first floor across the street. Overall, it was a net loss for them."

He moves to the suburbs next and it hits home as we've frequented the business he mentions on more than one Friday night.

"I talk to the guy with Little Ceaser's Pizza. All kinds of people told him to avoid downtown. They open up a location in West Lawn next to a Food Lion. The Food Lion closes after being open nine months." Val and I had shopped there a few times. "I get him into a location on Heister's Lane. In the first year they do $4 million in sales putting them in the top 10% in the entire company in terms of national sales. His biggest problem now? Some trash out front every now and then."

"You notice you don't see a Boscov's in the city? I've talked to his son-in-law. They have no interest in opening a store inside the city. You need to consider his 'investments' in the city. He can get $5 million in government tax credits and purchase them for $3 million. He can then write a check for the overflow and use it in a property as 'his own money.'"

I ask Shuman what Reading will look like in 2020.

"It depends on the elections. If we get Wally Scott and he turns out to be like the current administration, the city doesn't stand a chance. I'm lining up projects in the suburbs. I'm looking to fill 98,000 square feet of space right now that's sitting vacant. We need to create these jobs. That building at 8th and Oley can easily create sixty full time jobs. I'll get two projects like that a year."

Shuman uses his work to directly provide jobs in the community. His projects have offered employment to young people lacking other direction in their lives. They are proud of their work and he is glad to give it to them. He also opens his doors to volunteer groups and churches looking to help.

"From 2005-2007 we did an analysis of east coast cities all the way down to Mobile, Alabama. There was a bunch of Lehman Brothers money invested in Reading and we wanted to find the best way to handle it. In 2008, no city in the study was rated as high as

Reading for potential upside. Since then, Mobile has had $2.4 billion in development. They are a little bigger than Reading. Allentown as had $1 billion in development from the private sector because they were open to it. Reading isn't open to it."

The red tape can handicap any significant efforts and mire it in permits and procedures.

"Look at Boscov's hotel. That building is a $67 million hotel. With his tax credits and breaks, you're looking at a property worth at most $16 million for the city to tax, if it is actually on the tax rolls. If that went to me, I'd use it as a 20 % leverage on mortgages for new projects. I'd take that $67 million and turn it into $250 million easily. Reading could get 15,000 jobs over the next ten years and have millions in new tax revenues."

His expression turns wistful as he eases back in his chair.

"It is known that the city is dragging the entire county down with it. For 150 years Reading led the charge. It doesn't any more. In 2001, we tried building the Reading Railroad Museum in the city, you know, the city it was named after? I had it planned out. I had a company in France ready to come over the build an amusement park with it. We had all the specs mapped out. The city turned us down due to concerns with noise violations."

"I have a five year old son who loves trains and I need to drive him out to Hamburg to see the Reading Railroad Museum. It is crazy."

Shuman looks over his shoulder to a building that spans the length of the next city block.

"I sold that building for $6 million dollars. The owners want to sell it back to me for $2 million."

"A $4 million bath?" I ask.

"Yes, a $4 million bath." He points out another property in the distance, one with columns spanning the front.

"I'm about to purchase that from the owner. He had renovated the first three floors. The city came in and told him he needed to improve the fire safety measures on the upper floors, even though they were not occupied. He couldn't afford it, so it was abandoned."

Throughout our conversations, employees had left for the day and phone calls were answered in a distant office by an answering machine. Even in the space, papers, rain, massive conference table and all, I felt that Shuman cared. I had his attention. He was engaged and passionate.

"I want to turn this city around for my two kids so some day they can see the fruits of my efforts. I want my investments to pay off."

As I rise and we shake hands again, I believe him. He easily has the resources to leave the city and move to the suburbs. He could pick and choose his work at will and he remains here, in this land of politics, poverty, and people fighting to survive.

I push in my chair and back away from the table, leaving the left side slightly out from flush. He steps forward and completes the move, lining it up with the other chairs. That focus, care and concern for the small things is what may shift the future to the way it should be.

I exit the boardroom, now shadowed in corners, and Shuman disappears into an office I do not see, back to work on his uphill battle to change a city and make a difference his kids can be proud of.

Chapter 24

Editor and Journalist Charles Gallagher

It takes a moment for my eyes to adjust to the dim light of *Divot's Bar and Grill* as I spot Charles Gallagher seated at a table with his back to a deck that overlooks an adjacent golf course. We are in the midst of Flying Hills, a residential area that functions like its own world with a school, businesses, apartments, houses, and a recreation center.

Gallagher had spent forty years as a reporter for the *Reading Eagle*, ending his career as managing editor in 2008. He still makes appearances on local television to discuss issues of the day. His eyes are sharp, his voice commanding and his presence still the captain of a newsroom, one that worked the city of Reading through a turbulent handful of decades.

"We always had race issues here. I was editor during the race riots of the 1970's when they closed the *House of Soul.*" The riots he references happened when a white administration moved to close an establishment that had served the black community. It escalated to the point of violence in multiple parts of the city. The images are chilling to consider with the recent events in Ferguson, Missouri and New York in late 2014 and early 2015.

The problems of race and inequality, certainly not unique to Reading, only add to the city's environment.

"The influx of Latinos totally changed the complexion of the city in the late 1980's. Initially, it was Eastern Europeans settled south of Penn Street. The Germans were north of Penn Street. The African-American population stayed around 11%. This story is really the story of every city. There are places like Reading across the country," Gallagher says.

Golf carts cross paths just outside our window. The waitress returns to deliver my side salad and we wait until she goes back to her rounds. Gallagher takes a sip of his drink.

"Retirement plans are killer for everyone. They need to be adjusted. My wife is a retired teacher. She paid in her third, the district provides a third, and the rest should come from the government. It's not the case anymore."

Considering the issue of schooling, I ask him about Reading School District. The district is a conduit for debate and disagreement and has its share of allies and detractors throughout the city.

"The problems at Reading High aren't as great as everyone imagined. It is a testing issue. Look at the cheating in Atlanta." A large group of teachers in the city of Atlanta had been convicted of cheating on their standardized tests. The scandal sent shockwaves through the national system of education. Gallagher believes the school district is a product of the times.

"There are less bad people now than there was. In the 1960's, we had a terrible drug culture. Organized crime and corruption were all over the city. There's no money left now to take so the organized elements have moved out."

Gallagher is a man of history. He was stationed at Andrews Air Force Base when President Kennedy was elected and had to march in the inaugural parade, eventually spending four years in the service. In his time at the newspaper, he had interviewed Richard Nixon during his run for the White House.

"My military experience shaped my writing," he tells me. In the years since, he has written some history, fiction, two musicals and two plays that found their way into theaters.

"The 1960's made this city into a different place. Losing the railroad hurt. Losing industry hurt. There was a rapid decay and we made too many mistakes. The Redevelopment Authority was a bad choice. We needed to maintain businesses and restaurants and draw the middle class in as much as possible."

Would the impending bankruptcy of Reading level the playing field or provide any value?

"Bankruptcy doesn't mean anything. Some businesses have survived and will survive, places like *Judy's on Cherry* and the

Peanut Bar. We need to bring more into these places. Will that new hotel (DoubleTree on Penn Street) even have that much influence?"

I ask his opinion on the county commissioners, led by Christian Leinbach. Their office faces an uphill battle.

"The Commissioners are doing a great job. In the 1970's, things didn't get done. The county has ignored the city and wanted it to go away and vice versa. The current guys are very balanced."

I mentioned a speech given by Mayor Vaughn Spencer where he rallied against the county, saying residents could "take back the city." Gallagher laughs.

"Take it back from whom?" He asks me.

We finish our lunch as the rain picks up outside. The bottom line is, how do we change the impression of Reading that keeps visitors out and the darkness in?

"People are afraid of the city. Businesses are suffering because people are scared to come in. We need to remove that mentality. Change is not happening. It's part of the Pennsylvania

German ethic. You ever hear the joke, how many Berks County people does it take to change a light bulb?"

"How many?" I ask.

"Change?" Gallagher replies and laughs. "The important thing is that we have a consistent effort with the willingness to change. The same track will always lead to the same end point."

The check arrives and Gallagher pays for us both.

"Reading never really looked at poverty before. I remember when Hope Rescue Mission had thirty guys living there. The entire perception of the city must change or it won't get better. Reading needs a transfusion. Penn Street needs to be viable again."

As we leave lunch, I thank Gallagher for his input. His eyes for storytelling are still open and his instincts are sharp. This city must learn from the past, and its stories, if it will get back to life again.

Chapter 25

Lunch with Robert Turchi, Hope Rescue Mission

"See, I'm used to mine dripping."

Turchi pours an extra side of Thousand Island dressing on his Rueben sandwich. "Down in Philly, they came that way."

We sit in the dining room of the West Reading Tavern. The building is a central unit in a row of businesses, a bar and dining area fit inside a space less than ten paces wide. It calls back to a different, and older, time.

Turchi, tall and bald with a goat-tee just showing hints of grey, is a former court-appointed criminal investigator from Philadelphia. He grew up in Baltimore, moving to Philadelphia when he was eighteen years old. He met his wife, a social worker of Peruvian descent, in the city. After ten years of investigative work with the police department and Philadelphia court system, Turchi uprooted his family to head to "the country."

"It was a hard few years," he tells me, "We had seven officers die in that time span. Seven in the line of duty, not counting the ones who had committed suicide or things like that." Turchi entered full time ministry and assisted as chaplain. "It was hard reconciling my faith and the police work. I thought I'd be a light there, but it wasn't easy."

It took an introduction by a fellow church member to find Hope Rescue Mission. In his five years of employment, Hope has doubled its budget and impact in the community. There was a point where the 80,000 plus square foot building would hold seventy-five guys at a time. Now they'll see almost two hundred men at the peak of the Code Blue winter program.

Turchi is a relatively new guy in Berks County, living here for five years. The disconnection is a valuable starting point and different than many of the politically and historically vested individuals I've met so far.

"Is there a system in place that prevents success?" Turchi asks me. "Government support and care is a newer concept. In the last seventy years or so we've shot to a primary position in the issue. A lot has changed. The changes were good to a large degree. Now, the New Deal morphed into something holding down communities."

There is a seismic difference between a receiver and a creator. How does a city shift from receiving to creating? The bigger question is: are there people in Reading who want to be shifted?

"There may be agencies in the city that are comfortable. We'd rather stay out of politics. We want to be accountable to our supporters, not government money. Less government money equals more genuine support." Many outreach agencies are indebted to state and federal monies for their existence. If one can exist without it, there is freedom and validation of the work. It is a goal that Hope strives towards daily.

I had interviewed a young man living at the Mission for a news article. He mentioned a fine balance, that there were genuine people in charge of Hope. If you were straight with them, they would be straight with you and help. If you lied, the man told me, you were out the door. I mention the conversation.

"We're always gracious to people. There are few guys we wouldn't accept back. Some come and go and, unless you are being belligerent or something like that, we're there for you. We want to help them change and that only happens from within."

This internal change is necessary and, perhaps, the largest stumbling block. In an area with strong Pennsylvania Dutch roots, "change" is almost profanity. People here grasp onto an identity and refuse to let it go.

"There's a big difference between here and Philly. When we were there, people loved the city. There were plenty of cops who loved the city. They took pride in what they did. It's totally different here. People in Berks County hate Reading right now. We could get millions in government funding. Will it really change anything?" Turchi asks me.

In a city with this population, a small amount of government money goes a long way. It can be a prime laboratory for programs to combat poverty.

"If you think about it, there's no reason for struggle or poverty if government money solved anything," Turchi tells me as he cuts through the remaining half of his Rueben.

There is one element of the population that could stand up and shift things. The Latino community in the city is strong and growing. Every area of Central, South America, Puerto Rico, the Dominican Republic, and Mexico is represented. Even if the families come second generation from New York, they are growing by the year.

Turchi identifies a complication from this situation.

"Did you see that article talking about the school district? 71% of the students there claim Spanish is the first language spoken at home. Now, I lived and worked in Spanish-speaking countries. There is a certain community feel they bring over to this country. It must be worked with."

Poverty is subjective across the world. What is poor in Reading is not poor in the heart of Africa. Poor in the urban centers of Mexico is different on its own and it is a strong force of influence. Any native incoming people carry in their cultural traditions. If poverty makes the trip, it can take hold in the newest stop.

"How do we come alongside these families and help out? When multiple generations are in government programs, are we moving forward?"

Turchi's roots go back to Italy. His family was poor and uneducated. No one, he tells me, made it with government programs. They fought through learning trades and employment, eventually heading to schools. The family eventually found their foothold.

The deeper question is assimilation. Turchi believes Reading must be Reading, not small parts of Mexico, Puerto Rico, or other influential territories. Change may mean letting go of what was left behind and adapting more of a new way of life.

The Mission is still successful in the midst of this turbulence.

"First off, we honor the Lord and seek his blessing. We're a large facility. We're connected to all the local churches and we're easy to get into. Take a program like Teen Challenge." Teen Challenge works specifically with teens and addiction issues, "Teen Challenge is difficult for a guy on the street, in crisis, to get into as they have a high level of a required intake process. All you have to do is walk through our door. I mean, we have something everyone can support. Who wouldn't want to help the homeless? Fight hunger?"

The waitress arrives to take my plate with the remains of a turkey club. The small dining area had filled in around us and I lean in to hear our conversation. Turchi is softer-spoken, an advantage for a man with ministry in his soul and a contrast as a father of four kids all in elementary school. He is empathetic, a quality honed from years as an investigator, and he measures his words.

"There is too much of an 'us versus them' mentality, producer versus consumer." The Mission fights to break that cycle. Men must contribute to daily operations from their first day of residency. It is a two-fold effect. First, they are given responsibility and self-worth. Secondly, it weeds out guys who are just looking for a place to sleep and not see real change in their lives.

The environment in the city spurs conflict between charities and agencies fighting for their share of federal monies. Hope stands in a unique position. Donors are approaching with offers and support. Turchi's daily responsibilities have shifted mostly to the associate director, Frank Grill, and Chaplain Steve Olivo.

"I'm more of a marketing guy now. I get out and talk with donors, churches, and businesses. I can meet people and get our information out there."

He's doing this job particularly well. Wells Fargo, Turchi tells me, had just called to donate three separate properties, free and clear of debt, and contribute $10,000 for renovation costs.

Plans are forming to expand operations.

"We'd like to take one and make it into a Hope House for women and children," Turchi says. Grill, his associate director, had told me in our last meeting that supporters are prepped and excited about supporting a Hope branch for women. They had promised donations above and beyond their current engagement.

"The other, we'd like to see for 18-24 year old men. They need their own space. They're still kids. It would benefit them to be out of the main building to have their own level of support." Both of the Hope Houses would serve as transitional housing and would be staffed by guys who had gone through the Mission's programs and were deemed reliable and clean from addictions.

It is an effective formula. Not every guy at Hope will stay and work for there but, if they have the chance to get back on their feet, it is a serious opportunity.

The waitress arrives with our check. The dark dining room stands cool compared to the afternoon outside that is sunny and near 90 degrees. Summer, it seems, has come early in Reading.

"Summer is a chance to breathe. Our largest and most demanding program (Code Blue) closes down and we have some space. It's a good feeling."

We finish our drinks and Turchi pauses a moment, his mind still working over parts of our conversation. He looks at me.

"Here's a question you should ask. What is the advantage of being poor for the city? There's a lot of government money coming into a city of 90,000 people. Certain programs have a need to be filled for them to get government support. There's a program for apartment vouchers that requires forty people to be enrolled. If they get to a point with less than forty, the money goes away."

We make our way back to the street and the sun. I thank Turchi for his openness to talk and for Hope to be the first resource willing to address the story of poverty in Reading.

"See, a few years ago, you wouldn't have been called back. We're focused on staying open to the community. We're open to the community and taking calls from anyone."

Shoppers make their way to the cafés on Penn Avenue, carrying bags from the boutique stores that line the street. Just over the hill sits the Penn Street Bridge, a stretch of road connecting the inner city to this block of suburban life.

"You know what they call that bridge?" Turchi asks me, "the longest bridge in the state."

I jog across the intersection to the front of the Fred Astaire Dance Studio, cross one more time and walk to the parking lot that flanks Superior Oxygen, a Sunoco gas station, and a uniform store. Diners seated at outside tables watch the traffic pass. As I drive back towards the city I cross the bridge and, for a moment, the sun creeps back under a bank of passing clouds.

Chapter 26

Berks Coalition to End Homelessness Site Visit

The most noticeable aspect of the Salvation Army building at 301 South 5th St in Reading is the parking area. I had met Sharon Parker, head of the Berks Coalition to End Homelessness, about six months before at Barnes and Noble. This would be my first venture to her home turf.

The parking lot I'd expected to use was fenced off and totally inaccessible from the street with large NO PARKING signs on the fence. I pull my car across the street and enter the building, dodging two people in mid conversation on the steps.

The lobby is painted bright yellow, enough that any additional encroachment from the sun would have rendered it instant headache material. A handful of people wait in the chairs, eying me with appraising glances. Resources are available here for those in need, from physical to financial help. It takes a minute for a younger woman to appear at the desk. I tell her I am there to see Sharon. She makes a phone call as I wait.

The entrance to the sanctuary is to the right of the reception desk. The room is dark woods and purple carpeting, with crosses and bibles located in different spots, a constant reminder of the original goal that gave the Salvation Army the first word in its name.

"Matt? You can follow me." A woman with blonde, curly hair and glasses walks across the waiting room and I follow.

She uses her badge to buzz me into the gym. The building had once been an elementary school and I could hear the ghosts of kids playing tag, dodgeball, and shooting at the lowered basketball nets. After climbing two flights of stairs, we enter the coalition's office space.

It consists of two rooms painted white and three desks. Parker's office is in the back and she waves through the open door. The air conditioner is above my right shoulder and I spend our conversation with a frozen pen in hand.

"We've had this place since January of 2013," Parker tells me. She looks small behind her desk, an L shaped angle of wood with a computer, printer, folders, and a variety of papers.

Recent conversations had drifted around a concept of Housing First, created to push the homeless into residencies they may not be ready for and worry about cleaning up the other issues later.

"Housing First is great is a program, not a concept." It had started in the late 1980's. "It wants to bypass the shelter system and put people in apartments before handling any other needed services. It is great for episodic homelessness with normal stability. It doesn't work for everyone."

The program takes a large amount of public housing. The city of Reading does not have the assets for it to work and placing an addict or unstable person in a room before handling any wrap around services can be a recipe for disaster.

"Imagine being a landlord. I come to you and say, hey, here's a guy who is an addict, a hoarder, and paranoid. Give him a room and I'll be back to check on him every now and then. Don't worry, I'll pay for it," Parker says. Too often, homelessness and poverty combines with other issues that shelter and transitional housing can handle these before returning the individuals to society.

Parker is the point person for homelessness in Berks County. It is not the easiest job with the transient nature of the population, help, resources, and funding. She operates on a $120.000 operating budget, receiving state and federal grant monies to handle the overhead. I ask her about the bottom line that seems to be getting deeper with each passing month.

Is there any advantage to the city staying poor?

"It is a great question," Parker says and pauses. "From a nonprofit standpoint, I'd say no. Our world is reactionary. We can't stop the issues, only react to them. I'd love to be able to stop homelessness altogether. I'd love to not need to work this job ever again. There's a need for our programs and we must keep expanding."

The talk of expansion leads to the issues that come with it. With places like Hope Rescue Mission and the Coalition looking to expand their reach and obtain properties, they'll need to cut through the large and slow political red tape.

"Why should people have to wait?" Parker asks me. "There is no reason the coding department should be this slow. Look at the Water Authority situation." The Water Authority was a battle ground over the unions and local labor officials. The mayor stands in the middle, accused by many as being a union loyalist to the extent of handicapping expansion.

The primary elections in the city had just ended a week before. I ask Parker if she needs a Democratic administration to function well. The business leaders in the private sector staunchly disagree as they cry for change.

"It helps. I'm not political in this job but, with the democrats, the money flows much easier than with the republicans. I see both sides though. We need new businesses, like the hotel on Penn Street, to employ these people." It is a fine balance.

"Did you see that article about Allentown?" Parker asks me.

Besides the subject of the Billy Joel song, Allentown sits a few miles to the north and east of Reading. For years it was the home of Bethlehem steel and other industrial pursuits. It collapsed with the loss of industry and, according to the *Reading Eagle*, is now a place of development in action. Alan Shuman, CEO of Shuman Development Group, had mentioned Allentown to me during our interview as an example of a city open to private sector money.

"I called my friend that lives up there. He picks up the phone and I ask him how it is and tell him about this glowing write up in the paper. He laughed and said that it is still the same. The people still see it the same way it was before. You see, the city is the people."

The economists can do what they want, the politicians can play with pension funds and union contracts, the outreach programs can serve and expand but the people will always be the city. All the money and programs in the world won't change anything if the people don't make the choice to be different, to get up and move forward.

So what happens with a change in administration, I ask.

"I go and get them to like me again, go buy some cake or something. I'll head to city hall and present what we do all over again. I'll present our value. Fixing the city needs to be a number one priority. Changing the people is not easy when so many are a transient population. They aren't from here and they have no intent in staying here. We know that services will get cut over time and that we'll need to fight for funding again. We can't depend on the government."

Parker's cell phone rings and she answers it. She is getting a new chimney liner put in at her house, a lot that sits on the side of Neversink Mountain. We agree to end the interview a few minutes early.

"Poverty is not a choice anymore. You must do more for yourself. We need to get people out one at a time. Government help is not the answer. All we do is try to help as many people as we can, from coordinating services to making phone calls."

I follow Parker out to the massively secured parking area. We agree to keep in touch and I jog across the street, freeing up my parking spot for a waiting late model Toyota. I turn down the next street to find myself face to face with a pair of police cars dealing with a tan pickup truck and a driver with no shirt on. I swing a turn and backtrack to the highway and my way home.

Val tells me that the news has a story about a shooting in the city this morning. A man was asked if he had a cigarette by another man in a car. When he said he did not, he was shot and killed. Parker's comments replay in my head.

Can the choices needed to make a difference ever happen in reality? Not if people are being shot over cigarettes. The battle, and the fight for authentic change, will continue.

Chapter 27

Family Promise of Berks County

I pass it twice before pulling over on 5th street and starting the GPS on my phone. The office for Family Promise is a unit in a historical section of row homes in the city. I park next to a pair of black trash bags waiting for pickup and make my way across the street.

Family Promise is a national organization that started in New York City originally to help serve the community of elderly poor and homeless. It expanded to 190 affiliates in forty-five states with the office in Reading now open for a decade.

I follow a family up the stairs to the main office to meet Gwen Didden, a "recovering minister's kid," and the executive director of the organization's Berks County office. The layout of the building is almost identical to Mercy Pregnancy Center, with Didden's office taking place of Mercy's Community Room. I take a seat across a circular table covered with a tablecloth fitting a summer barbeque.

"I got tipped off to the headline (Reading as the poorest city in the United States) a few days before it broke, so I was ready. It was an exhausting time. I got calls from the U.K. and France, from news agencies across the country looking for information. The magazine in France sent a film crew here to take footage and shoot interviews. The world descended on Reading. We became the face of poverty," Didden tells me.

A construction crew rips into the street outside, diggers and saws punctuating our conversation.

"We were used to the flow of people. When the bubble burst in 2008, 09, 10, the middle class dropped away. We do things like rental assistance for the middle class. After the dust settled in 2011 we had a new working poor." Didden's Master's degree in Human Service hangs on the wall. Her passion is understanding poverty and homelessness. The events of most recent recession of 2008 had placed her in the perfect position. She had taken the job as director just three years after the founding of the Reading office.

"I originally ran from here. I did a few different things, I ran Beacon House. I had a job in the city but was miserable. God kept drawing me back. I wanted a job I didn't have to work at. The board here finally called me and left me a voicemail offering the job. The first year was a challenge. We had to bring it all to zero and start fresh."

In a city with a world of charities fighting over limited funds, not every organization took the chance to make it happen. The ones that failed fell away.

"The morning we were supposed to have layoffs, I remember driving in here stressed out. I had a phone call from the wife of a local businessman. He had $12,000 to donate and she wanted to know if we could use it. The county called us and said they had some stimulus money left and wanted to know if we could use a little over $310,000. The next year, they had more than $200,000 to donate. We've never had to shut the lights off, lay off anyone, or close our doors," Didden says.

The process for a family to enter the Family Promise program is strenuous but valuable. They must complete a twelve page application, vetted by staff members, and a background check. The family takes a tour and both staff and family must agree that the program is a fit after a twenty-four hour period of consideration. It is an intensive experience. Families are housed in local churches and given support and resources for daily life and getting back on their feet, including showering at the Family Promise office. They can only go through the program one time but, after completion, they are always welcomed to contact staff and use available resources and there are never more than three families in the program at one time.

At the moment, they'll move fifteen families through the program out of 200 applications for the year.

"Those in homelessness need a spiritual awakening. I believe in what we are doing here. It works because these people are surrounded by God's people. Homelessness is not about money, it is about a soul sickness. If they find healing, the rest will fall into place. It wouldn't work any other way. We help those in need to get back on track," Didden says.

With the sheer volume of applications, there are additional programs available.

"There are programs for addiction and mental health problems. We offer prayer, referrals, anything needed from the application. We trust the process and help out with the leg work. I was a single mom on welfare. I remember how it was. We like to say that nobody leaves here without hope. The truth will always come out and light shines through the darkness."

Didden believes that there is no short term fix for homelessness. Family Promise can only start people on track towards success and breaking the cycle.

"You must apply the science to it. You'll cause harm if you don't know what you're doing."

I was told, by Sharon Parker at the Coalition to End Homelessness, to ask Didden about the Palace Project. When I mention it, her eyes light up. She takes a breath and carries me on an expansive narrative.

"In August 2012, I knew there had to be something more than this and started asking God about it. In October, God had me start a forty-day fast. I went to Glad Tidings (church) after this. Now, I'd always seen things, even as a little girl. I went to the prayer rooms at Glad Tidings to get some clarity. I even traveled up to the chapel at Blue Mountain."

The construction sounds continue outside. A trash truck slowly makes its way past our windows.

"I had a vision of this river on a sunny afternoon with lines of beach chairs and people next to it. Jesus appeared at my side and told me it was the River of Life. He said that everyone likes to be near it but nobody wants to jump in. I decided, from there on, I'd jump in and never get out."

This was March, 2013. Didden continues, the words flowing freely, punctuated by an easy smile.

"I received the vision for the Palace Project, wrote it all down, and backed it up with Scripture."

The main thrust of the Project is about obedience, something necessary for combatting personal, spiritual, and societal ills.

"Obedience is the key to higher living. God told me that I needed to stop using the words believers and unbelievers. From here on out, there is only believers and *future believers.*" Her eyes widen. "I didn't like the name originally but God confirmed it. There is one palace in Heaven, the scripture says, with many rooms." It is a unique path, suited to a women focused on getting people homes in the earthly and spiritual realms.

"Family Promise in Reading is run differently. I believe God will pay for what he orders. I won't compromise or play the game. I always said we are 49% business and 51% ministry. When that ratio flips, then there is a problem. We need to create new missionaries to invade the systems, not societies. God will get the glory in his time. We bring the mission field directly to the churches. We take the souls there for hands-on ministries."

Didden's path hadn't always been easy or clear. She tells me that one day she had lunch with a board member of another local organization. The woman offered her a position with a hefty salary. It would have been easy to take.

"I could have retired there. I asked God what I should do. He said that the enemy was playing Let's Make a Deal. The same day I received an email invitation to preach in Kenya. Since then I've been to Kenya, India, and Europe multiple times."

After God's promise of a world audience, Didden says she is amazed at how it played out. At a conference on poverty held in Amsterdam, she was seated at a table with a CEO and two high-ranking members of the European Union.

"The world systems are flawed but his systems are flawless. As I was going home from Amsterdam I said to God, send me anywhere but India. The first call I received when I got home was from a ministry in India with an invitation to preach."

The Palace Project is now building an orphanage in India under the arm of their nonprofit agency. They are helping to run a women's conference for ministry in Kenya, where Didden was invited to preach on a national television program. The churches in these countries are hungry for encouragement and support.

"This is a deep transformational process. It took the Apostle Paul thirteen years to get there. Not everyone goes through it. I believe political will and social justice go hand in hand. We faced some tough oppression in both places. In India, anyone declaring themselves Christian is automatically placed in the lowest caste. It costs $25.00 to feed a family for a month there. I believe India will be a Christian nation one day."

The Project has also set up an account to pay the rent for a school in Kenya. It can provide for all needs for $60.00 a month plus a food stipend.

"Our ceiling is their floor," Didden says, "our nets are broken."

One of the ways to fix these "nets" is a return to creativity.

"Creativity is coming back. We were told, by God, to make a documentary, to get a film crew together and go on the streets and ask people one question; *what do they think of Christians*? We are to go to the churches and play the results. We'll see if we are ready to have that honest conversation then. We'll see if we are ready for the souls who are coming."

The Project is setting up an online store for crafts, shirts, books, and other devotional materials. Didden is excited about the prospects of this outreach. Her personality and dreams overflow the confines of the office.

I ask what can be done to change the soul of Reading.

"We need to pay attention to the character of our politics. People must take pride in ownership and that is missing right now. If the heart is corrupted there will be corruption in the system. There needs to be a shift in political will. Believers need to invade the systems. Did you know there is a Bible study in the Senate? We need to see that kind of thing here or they'll be no change."

I check the clock hanging over Didden's shoulder. We'd been talking for almost two hours.

"We must set boundaries and generate trust. Who can we trust with the heart and soul of the city? There's so much corruption here. If we do nothing, we are part of the problem. We need new missionaries, ordinary people with extraordinary faith. God is calling people and not all will respond. Nonprofits applications have increased here by 25% a year. The political will always follows social justice. Churches are losing money. They need mature leaders to step up and take the hit."

Didden asks me if she can pray for this book and our efforts. We close our eyes and I listen as she entreats God on our behalf for inspiration, direction, and impact.

As I leave the building, I notice I was wrong. The trash had not been picked up. Even with all the noise of construction, it still remained, the smell pushed by a breeze down the streets. I go do drive away and a city bus blocks my exit as it drops off passengers in front of me and, for the moment, I'm stuck.

Chapter 28

Summer

"I needed this," I say, looking across the baseball fields. I stand next to Dan Clouser on a warm afternoon in June. Clouser, the founder of the Big Vision Foundation and Berkshire Baseball, had just finished a lesson with Carter. We were a few weeks into our lessons and he loved coming out to learn and watch baseball.

The Big Vision Complex is just off Route 183, a few miles north of Reading. It houses Charlie Wagner Field, named after the Berks County native who played his career with the Boston Red Sox. The field is a replica of Fenway Park, including a smaller version of the notorious Green Monster wall in left field.

Clouser is a big man, sure spoken yet with softness in his voice. He had coached for decades, winning more than a thousand games at the youth level including a stint working for the

Philadelphia Phillies as an associate scout. After founding Berkshire Baseball with a group of friends, it has grown into a force on the baseball scene, holding numerous tournaments and events. It offers lessons, family movie nights, concessions, and four manicured baseball fields. Clouser's efforts generate more than $7 million in income for Berks County every year.

"I know everyone grieves differently," Clouser says to me. We shake hands as Carter collects the baseballs in the hitting cage.

The day before the lesson, I was getting a shower when Val burst into the bathroom.

"I can't breathe," she said in a panic.

I asked what happened and she told me.

Pastor Bryan Koch, head of our home church and a man I interviewed for this book was in a motorcycle accident that morning with his wife Lynn. She had died at the scene and he was in intensive care at Reading Hospital after a leg amputation and numerous internal injuries.

The news sank into my chest.

I went to work having my own issues thinking and functioning. Around noon the same day I received a text message. My grandmother, Hazel Shaner, had passed away in the hospital after 99 years of life.

It was too much.

I watch Carter hit. He's like a machine, the metal bat pinging baseball bullets back into the net. Before every pitch, Carter resets himself and I have a vision of him ten years in the future, for death always makes you aware of life and what is standing in front of you.

"Did you see that Facebook conversation?" Clouser asks me. I tell him that I did.

Big Vision was the subject of a glowing post by Craig Poole, manager of the new DoubleTree hotel in the city. Poole had been amazed as the sheer scope of what Big Vision did on a daily basis. In the comment thread, multiple people theorized on where they could open a complex like Big Vision in the city. It went on and on until Clouser chimed in.

Guys, we already have it. We are here. We just need help from the community to take it to the next level.

"I'm glad you said something, because I was going to if you didn't," I tell him.

"You know what it would take to do something like this from scratch? $30 million easy. Now, you'll find communities who are willing to spend that on a sports complex, but not here. We need $7 million to complete all the renovations I'd like to see," Clouser says.

"That's less than half." I do the math.

"Exactly."

Carter takes his glove out of his bag and starts throwing a ball in the air. In a game on a distant field, one of the players hits a homerun and the crowd cheers as he jogs around the bases.

I spend the next few days glued to my phone searching for updates on Bryan's condition. On Wednesday night that week, our church holds a prayer service and more than 1,500 people attended. Bryan's personal and professional friends offer condolences and prayers. We sing and profess our faith at something better. We may get knocked down but, one day, we'll get back up again.

As Val and I sit in the stadium seating, I look across the rows below me. All ages, income levels, and ethnic groups are here. The community had come out in support of those facing this tragedy. Other clergy sit to our right. The church had received support messages from across the world.

Scott Kramer, executive pastor of Glad Tidings, takes the stage surrounded by the five member elder board. For a moment, there is no agenda, no politics, talk of money or procedures. There is unity.

"I grabbed that left arm, that throwing arm of the former MLB catcher, and squeezed it and told him how much I loved him and missed him," Kramer says, "and he opened his eyes and looked at me."

The crowd erupts.

"Dad can you throw to me?" Carter asks.

I say I would and we have a catch on the hill overlooking the baseball fields. The lesson had just finished. We schedule the next one and Clouser drives away on a golf cart.

We have a catch for a few minutes and walk over to watch the games. I answer every question he has about baseball. The summer breeze, constantly crossing the fields from the surrounding mountains, pushes against our faces. Carter reclines in the grass.

There is something in the snap of the mitts, the crack of the bats, and the smell of freshly grilled hamburgers at the concession stands. I think of the intersection of years, the crossing of time when old gives way to new.

I think of losing the last of my grandparents.

"Are we going to back away or move forward?" Pastor Phil Baker asks the crowd. Baker, a relatively new addition to the staff, strides across the stage to cheers. I think of my interview with Bryan. He had been open, honest and forthcoming. He had listened to my questions and was more than generous with his answers. He had promised we would meet again in the future to check in.

Now he was in critical condition.

Something he said during our interview came back.

"We asked people in the area what they thought about us, what they knew about GT. They said we were the big church. That really bothered me. I don't want us to be known as the big church. I want us to be known as the church that made a difference in the community."

I look at the crowd and believe he will see it happen. This packed church is a glimpse of the solution, the chance to change things for the better. Part of me believes that Koch would understand and know that his suffering had become a catalyst towards the movement he desired, one that could impact this city and this area for years to come.

Breaking the Jar

How do we change a city? When the idea for this book hatched, I held onto two points. First, I wanted the words to make a difference. Secondly, I had known the headline naming Reading the poorest city in the United States in 2011. With these in mind I set out contacting resources. The journey led me across a city, from the streets to the hallways of power. I talked to the homeless, those running charities, religious leaders, and decision makers. Throughout the interviews, a story emerged.

The size and shape gradually became evident.

The final result isn't clear or easy.

When I started this process, every idea sounded like the solution. From Brian Kelly and his alternative economy to Craig Poole walking Penn Street in an effort to change the city one business at a time, every hand in the pot seems a valuable contribution.

The first issue is identifying the problem. Reading has flipped the jar on itself and, whether a victim of tangible forces or external prejudices, the jar hasn't moved. Those struggling with homelessness, poverty, illness and mental instabilities will continue to be an issue as the city attempts to produce services to handle these individuals. Combine this with the flight of industry outside the city borders and you have a perfect storm that swirls over the abandoned factories, antique buildings, courthouse, and small businesses that line the streets.

When I would tell a friend that I was headed to Reading to interview someone, I would get the same expression and warning. Be careful. Lock your doors. Watch your surroundings.

The second issue is ending this perception.

Peter Barbey told me that there is a certain "Berks County" feel to this area. It is the German attempt to avoid change as long as possible, even when presented with the truth. Charles Gallagher told me a joke.

"How many people in Berks County does it take to change a lightbulb?"

"How many?" I asked.

"Change? What's that?" he replied.

It may sound like an exaggeration, but it is not far from the truth. The view of a city is intrinsic as much as reality-based. If Reading does turn itself around, will it be embraced? Can the city stand up under the impression of those inside and around it?

The solution to finally shatter the glass jar will come in a collective effort across organizations, politics, and neighborhoods. On the street, it will take a consolidation of service agencies to finally stop fighting for funds and start communicating. In business, it will take learning, planning, spending, and a sense of civic pride.

The political side may be the hardest function to crack and change. The city of Reading was influenced by the heavy hands of unions and organized crime for years. You paid to play for a long time and the reach of corruption may not be so far in the past.

The bottom line is an issue of faith spread throughout every cog and gear that makes the city function. It is shared between every employee, from the street to the boardroom. Every resident must believe in something better, take pride in what they have, and fight to move forward.

It takes faith to grasp a city and call it your own, to create a mix of ethnic backgrounds and celebrate every single one. It takes belief in the human spirit to life heads above the grasp of poverty, to use anger and disappointment as motivation and create a sense of accountability that spans time and space.

It takes faith for every new small business to open its doors in the city and every major player in the corporate world to take a shot and put down roots. You can see it in the faces of those fighting on a daily basis. You see it in the cafeteria of Hope Rescue Mission on Thanksgiving and the hands of volunteers from the Greater Berks Food Bank giving out bags of food to school students every week.

You see it in those who are ready, from Craig Poole and his hotel to Dan Clouser and his baseball and sports complex, from Sherry Camellerri at Mercy Pregnancy Center helping those just born to Sheriff Eric Weaknecht and his goal to open the hands of city policing.

I'll acknowledge that this book is, by no means, the entire story. There are many organizations who had ignored my requests for interviews, and that is fine. There are many voices with something to say who may feel slighted by this text.

The answer is simple.

Get involved. Have the hard conversations. Walk the streets.

I know now that my conversation with Peter Barbey has held true, that this is not just the story of Reading. This was never totally about poverty. It was about the fight to survive, to live another day and redefine an identity in a post-industrial society. It was about the families struggling to make it after an economy had shattered, throwing people on the street with no job and no means to find one.

This was not just the story of Reading.

This is the story of every city.

This is every glass jar city waiting to be shattered and the gathering of enough force to finally break free.

Winter 2016

I sit across from Dan Clouser inside *The Van Reed Inn*, working on their fried shrimp special as he sampled the boneless wings. We were catching up from the summer. I'd followed Big Vision's efforts on social media. They were organizing and preparing for a new season.

"Was there ever a point where you looked in the mirror and questioned what you were doing?" I asked.

He laughed.

Two years before, Berks County had cut funding from his group, in a move never fully explained. Clouser was almost three decades into serving the community.

"One of my mentors told me that we needed to keep going, keep doing what was important. Sandy and I looked in the mirror and knew we were in it together."

Things have changed since the start of this book. Vaughn Spencer is no longer mayor of Reading, losing an election to follow democrat Wally Scott. Craig Poole's hotel is up and running, a new social center in the city. Hope Rescue Mission has started a capital campaign to raise funds for a needed renovation with, coincidentally, Poole as manager.

Brian Kelly's efforts have expanded and earned recognition.

Pastor Bryan Koch has recovered and returned to church. He walks with a prosthetic leg and preaches with more fire and conviction than ever before. Christian Leinbach, unlike Spencer, was elected for an additional term as County Commissioner. Eric Weaknecht also earned another run as sheriff.

Peter Barbey has purchased *The Village Voice* through his investment company. He continues to lead *The Reading Eagle*. Reading still sits under Act 47 and only time will tell if it recovers.

The story grows and changes. Violence is still a factor and has crept inside the walls of the school district. Families attempt to stand together and find an answer.

Those in this book fight the battle on a daily basis. They remain my heroes and inspiration. Their work deserves recognition and, one day, they will see their efforts rewarded as the city emerges in new and better life for every person who calls it home.

Acknowledgements

First, I want to thank my wife Valerie and my boys Carter and Aiden. I couldn't be a writer without their support and patience. Val you are an amazing wife and mother and I owe you more than I could ever put into words. I want to thank Colin Hosten and Jillian Ross, friends and fellow writers, for their input and direction.

Huge thanks to Pastor Brian Koch and the rest of our family at Glad Tidings Church in Wyomissing. Thank you for your spiritual guidance and leadership. To everyone who gave their time and efforts to let me hang out and hammer them with questions, I am in eternal debt.

Finally, to the fighters, to the ones who get up every morning and work against the tide of poverty and homelessness, this book is for you. May you always have the courage to wake up and do it again tomorrow.

"Trust in the Lord with all your heart and lean not on your own understanding. Submit to him in everything and he will make your paths straight." Proverbs 3:5-6

www.p356writing.com